# CHURCH ROOTS

## Charles P. Lutz, Editor
~Foreword by David W. Preus~

*Stories of Nine Immigrant Groups
That Became The American
Lutheran Church*

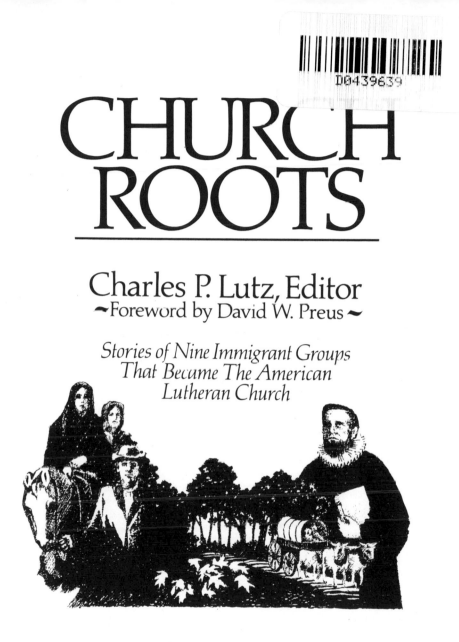

**AUGSBURG** Publishing House • Minneapolis

CHURCH ROOTS
**Stories of Nine Immigrant Groups That Became The American Lutheran Church**

Copyright 1985 Augsburg Publishing House

Scripture quotations unless otherwise noted are from the Revised Standard Version of the Bible, copyright 1946, 1952, and 1971 by the Division of Christian Education of the National Council of Churches.

**Library of Congress Cataloging in Publication Data**

Main entry under title:

CHURCH ROOTS.

    Bibliography: p.
    1. Lutheran Church—United States—Addresses, essays, lectures. 2. American Lutheran Church (1961- )—Addresses, essays, lectures. 3. United States—Church history—Addresses, essays, lectures. I. Lutz, Charles P. II. American Lutheran Church (1930-1960)
BX8041.C48 1985     284.1'31     85-1217
ISBN 0-8066-2156-7

Manufactured in the U.S.A.          APH 10-1366

1  2  3  4  5  6  7  8  9  0  1  2  3  4  5  6  7  8  9

# Contents

# Foreword

There are some grand stories from the 19th-century beginnings of The American Lutheran Church. They deserve to be better known. This volume tells nine of them in a way that makes history fascinating, fun, and pertinent to our time.

Here are stories of pioneer circuit-riding on the frontier, of jail terms for church leaders in Norway and Germany, of martyrdom for a missionary in Wyoming, of bungled colonizing in the independent Republic of Texas, of lockouts and lawsuits involving a church publishing house. And more.

Through all the stories, though, there are constant themes: the gospel is being preached, the church is being planted in a new land, the effort to share Christ with alien cultures is being made.

I find it fascinating that as far back as 1843 the three ethnic strains that would form The ALC 117 years later happened to come together for an ordination service in southeast Wisconsin. A young Dane, called to serve a group of Norwegian immigrants at Muskego, was ordained in a barn loft sanctuary by a German pastor.

The questions and issues with which our 19th-century prede-cessors struggled have not died. They sound very much like those that face us today. Thus, in addition to being good stories, these nine tales from the last century can help us with our search for faithful responses to God's call as we enter the closing years of our own century.

I welcome this collection especially as we celebrate a quarter century of life together in The American Lutheran Church and as we look forward to uniting with an even wider stream of U.S. Lutherans.

DAVID W. PREUS
Presiding Bishop
The American Lutheran Church

# Contributors

In nearly all cases, the writers of these stories are heirs of the traditions they describe. Three were born just after the 19th century closed. All have been around longer than The American Lutheran Church itself.

The writers are students of the church tradition which gave birth to them and have an obvious fondness for it. But, unlike many of our forebears in the 19th century, they are able to write with a certain detachment about the early days, allowing for discussion of weaknesses as well as strengths.

ALFRED H. EWALD was born in 1901. His father had Buffalo Synod background and his mother's origins were Missouri Synod. They were members of an Ohio Synod congregation in North Tonawanda, New York, where Alfred was baptized. He graduated from the Buffalo Synod's Martin Luther Seminary in 1923 and served as pastor of Hope Lutheran Church in St. Paul for the next 27 years. From 1950 to 1957 Dr. Ewald was president of the Minnesota District of the former American Lutheran Church. He was president of Wartburg Seminary, Dubuque, Iowa, from 1957 to 1967. He served as a member of the Joint Union Committee which prepared for the formation of the present ALC in 1960.

GRACIA GRINDAL was raised in a Lutheran Free Church parsonage. She is a member of the faculty of Luther Northwestern Theological Seminary, St. Paul, and has taught English at Luther College, Decorah, Iowa. She graduated from Augsburg College and received a Master of Fine Arts degree from the University of Arkansas. Ms. Grindal is the author of two poetry collections, *Pulpit Rock* and *Sketches Against the Dark*, and a book of sketches on Linka Preus to be published by the Norwegian-American Historical Association in cooperation with the Minnesota Historical Society. She also edits *Well Woman*, newsletter of the Lutheran Women's Caucus.

THEODOR I. JENSEN was born in 1901 and baptized in a United Danish Church congregation near Lindsay, Nebraska. After graduating from Trinity Seminary, Blair, Nebraska, he served congregations in Farmington, Minnesota, and Des Moines and Audubon, Iowa. He became professor of systematic theology at Trinity in 1944 and was one of three faculty members who moved with the seminary to the campus of Wartburg Seminary, Dubuque, Iowa, in the fall of 1956. He retired from teaching in 1971.

LEIGH D. JORDAHL, ALC pastor, was born in Decorah, Iowa. Both his grandfather and great-grandfather were pastors in the former Norwegian Synod. A graduate of Luther College in Decorah, Iowa, and Bethany Lutheran Seminary in Mankato, Minnesota, he also received a degree from Luther Theological Seminary, St. Paul, and a doctorate from the University of Iowa. Mr. Jordahl taught for 13 years at the Lutheran Theological Seminary, Gettysburg, Pennsylvania, and since 1977 he has served as head librarian and professor of religion and classics at Luther College.

CHARLES P. LUTZ is editor of this book and director of the Office of Church in Society, The American Lutheran Church. He is the great-grandson of an early Iowa Synod pastor, Friedrich Lutz, who began his studies at Wartburg Seminary the year it opened (1857) at St. Sebald, Iowa, and served the Iowa Synod as pastor, editor, professor, and college president, from 1863 until 1931. Charles is a graduate of Wartburg College, Waverly, Iowa, and Capital (now Trinity) Seminary, Columbus, Ohio.

FRED W. MEUSER is a son of Ohio and of the Joint Synod of Ohio. A church historian, he authored the history of the creation (1930) of the former American Lutheran Church. He joined the faculty of Capital (now Trinity) Seminary, Columbus, Ohio, in 1953, served as its president (1971-78), and has been president of Trinity since its founding in 1978.

TODD NICHOL serves as associate pastor at St. Philip Lutheran Church, Fridley, Minnesota. He has also taught church history at Luther Northwestern Theological Seminary. One of his grand-parents was a member of the United Norwegian Lutheran Church and he is a graduate of the college of which he writes (St. Olaf).

GERHARD M. SCHMUTTERER is professor of modern foreign lan-guages at Augustana College, Sioux Falls, South Dakota, where he has taught since 1953. Born in New Guinea to German Lu-theran missionary parents, he spent most of his childhood at Neuendettelsau, Germany. He received his B.A. at Augustana and his Ph.D. at the University of Erlangen.

ROLF A. SYRDAL was born in Hatton, North Dakota, in 1902 and was baptized in St. John's Lutheran Church, a congregation of the United Norwegian Lutheran Church. He and Mrs. Syrdal were missionaries in China, 1929-37. He wrote his Ph.D. dissertation (Drew University, 1942) on "American Lutheran Mission Work in China.'' Dr. Syrdal served parishes in Madelia, Minnesota; Brooklyn, New York; and Cedar Falls, Iowa. He taught at St. Olaf College, Luther College, and Luther Theological Seminary in St. Paul. He served as executive secretary for the Board of Foreign Missions of the Evangelical Lutheran Church from 1946 to 1960 and as director of world missions of The American Lutheran Church, 1961-62.

FRANK R. WAGNER was born in Bad Nauheim, West Germany. His wife Martina is a native of Basel, Switzerland. Both have visited nearby St. Chrischona and its mission school. A 1984 graduate of Trinity Seminary, Columbus, Ohio, Frank is assistant pastor at Lutheran Church of the Cross, St. Petersburg, Florida. He spent his seminary internship year at Zion Church, Fredericksburg, Texas, one of the pioneer congregations of the Synod in Texas.

# Acknowledgments

I wish to thank Professor James Limburg of Luther Northwestern Theological Seminary in a special way, since this project originated in a conversation the two of us enjoyed while driving across Nebraska after speaking to a pastors' conference in 1982. It was subsequently encouraged and assisted through conversations with several church historians: E. Clifford Nelson of St. Olaf College, Fred W. Meuser of Trinity Lutheran Seminary, and Eugene Fevold and James Nestingen of Luther Northwestern Seminary.

The genesis of the idea for such a collection of stories on the roots of The ALC, however, came because of the work of Gerhard M. Schmutterer, who teaches German at Augustana College, Sioux Falls, South Dakota. I was privileged several years ago to read his book-length manuscript on the Iowa Synod's dramatic efforts to evangelize Indians in Wyoming Territory, 1858-66 (see bibliography for Chapter 6). That reading suggested the possibility of a collection of briefer stories from the beginning years of each of the nine groups. This volume is the result.

Finally, I wish to thank the director of book development at Augsburg Publishing House, who liked the idea from the start and encouraged its development as a 25th anniversary gift to the people of The American Lutheran Church.

CHARLES P. LUTZ
Minneapolis

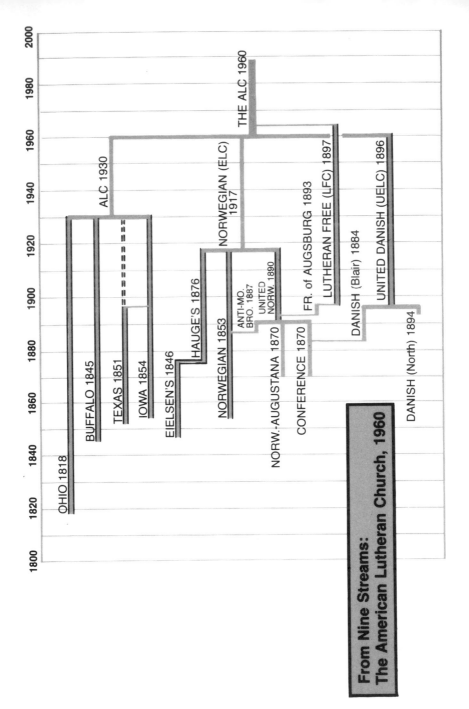

From Nine Streams:
The American Lutheran Church, 1960

# Introduction

by Charles P. Lutz

The 19th century was filled with beginnings for the Lutherans in the United States who eventually found their way into a single church family: The American Lutheran Church. This volume is about those beginnings—nine of them. The stories are told now as a recollection of the roots of The ALC.

As it observes its 25th anniversary in 1985, The American Lutheran Church also looks ahead to the formation of yet another Lutheran church body in the United States, yet another step in the two-century-old process of seeking to unify Lutherans in this nation. When The ALC looks ahead, it cannot help but look back as well—to its origins in the 19th century, to its roots in German and Norwegian and Danish immigrations. Chiefly, those immigrations had their destination in the middle part of this country—from Ohio west to Kansas and Nebraska, from Minnesota south to Texas.

Four of the synods whose stories appear took geographic names: Ohio, Buffalo, Texas, Iowa. They are the four churches of German origin. They did not, in the main, overlap much with one another, at least in the beginning.

It was quite different with the Norwegians. They also are represented by four stories. But they were born and spent their early years together in the same territory, chiefly a band of settlement from northern Illinois through southern Wisconsin and northern Iowa into southern and western Minnesota, the Dakotas, and eastern Montana. The Norwegian Lutherans of the four church varieties not only settled in the same region but also were often of the same families. They knew each other. Some had been acquainted already in Norway. The kinship among the Norwegian Lutherans in the United States meant there was always, from the beginning, a strong drive toward unity among them. It also meant their conflicts, like those in any family, were sometimes marked by a kind of personal bitterness that made reconciliation difficult.

The Danes were fewer in number than either the Germans or the Norwegians. They are represented by one story. The Danish immigration was not as large as that of the Norwegians and Germans, and not a very large proportion of the Danes who came here remained in the Lutheran church. Those who did organize into Lutheran congregations found themselves divided between two groups, a division that continues to this day. As the chapter on the United Evangelical Lutheran Church (UELC) explains, one of the gifts of the formation of a new Lutheran church by the end of this decade will be the uniting, at last, of the two Danish-American Lutheran streams.

### The 19th Century: Start to Finish

As the 19th century dawned, John Stauch, a Lutheran lay preacher located in Washington County, Pennsylvania, was making regular circuit rides into eastern Ohio to minister to Germans who had no pastors. From those scattered settlements, a first conference of Lutherans west of the Alleghenies was organized in 1812. Six years later, many of them would be part of the first Lutheran synodical body beyond the mountains and John Stauch, by now ordained, would become its first president.

As the 19th century ended, a group of Norwegian Lutherans in the Upper Midwest, who prized congregational freedom, were forming the Lutheran Free Church. Last of the nine groups to be organized (1897), the LFC was also the last to find its way into the present American Lutheran Church (1963).

Between the opening and closing decades of the century, seven other groups had their birth. Five of them came to life during one prolific decade right in the middle of the century, from Buffalo's formation in 1845 through Iowa's in 1854.

These nine churches came together in three stages. Step one occurred in the 1890s. One of the nine, the United Norwegian Church, was formed in 1890 by three small Norwegian groups. Another of the nine, the United Danish Church, emerged in 1896 from a union of two Danish synods. And two of the German synods, Iowa and Texas, formed a federation in 1897.

Step two came in the second and third decades of this century. First, in 1917, the majority of the Norwegians united in the Norwegian Lutheran Church of America (later renamed the Evangelical Lutheran Church). One group, the Lutheran Free Church, stayed outside. Then, the German-American bodies found each other in the former American Lutheran Church in 1930.

Finally, in 1960, strongly pushed by the Danish-background UELC, the former ALC and the ELC were ready to form the present ALC, the first major U.S. Lutheran merger across ethnic lines. The remaining Norwegian-origin group (LFC) entered three years later.

If all of this sounds complex, that is because it is. In fact, we have not mentioned all of the smaller splits and combinations that occurred along the way to eventual unity. (The diagram on page 12 may help to clarify things a bit.)

### Connections in the 1840s

While these groups of Lutherans would not officially unite until the 1960s, they had awareness of each other for more than a century before. The first formal connection should probably be counted as an ordination that happened in southeast Wisconsin on October 18, 1843. A 23-year-old Dane named Claus Laurits Clausen, who had a call from a Norwegian congregation at Muskego, was ordained in a barn loft sanctuary near Muskego by a German pastor of the soon-to-be-formed Buffalo Synod, L. F. E. Krause of Freistadt. Clausen's call is considered the birthdate of Norwegian-American Lutheranism.

It is fascinating that the three ethnic groups which would come together 120 years later in The American Lutheran Church were represented in that loft. And there was theological as well as ethnic diversity present on that October day in 1843.

> Krause was one of the founders in 1845 of the Buffalo Synod, which held an extremely high doctrine of the church and the ministry and claimed that outside the true, visible, orthodox Lutheran church there were only mobs and sects. The ordinand . . . was both a pietist and admirer of that creative genius, the Danish churchman, N. F. S. Grundtvig. Finally, the Norwegians among whom Clausen was to serve as pastor were Haugean Lutherans. High-church orthodoxy, genial Grundtvigianism, and evangelical pietism—all were present at that ordination service in Muskego's haymow temple.[1]

There would be other connections over the next dozen decades before these nine churches came together in one. Some were formal, such as their cooperation in common work through the National Lutheran Council (organized 1918) and the American Lutheran Conference (1930). Many were informal, such as the Norwegian Synod's exploration of possible use of the seminaries of Buffalo or Ohio for theological training (1855). (Instead, the Norwegian Synod chose to educate its pastors at the Missouri Synod's seminary in St. Louis, an arrangement that continued until the 1870s.)

There was even one proposal—as early as 1852!—to unite across ethnic boundaries. In that year, Pastor Adolph Carl Preus urged the leaders of what would in 1853 become the Norwegian

Synod to consider a proposal that the Norwegians unite with the Joint Synod of Ohio. The suggestion had been made by Professor W. M. Reynolds, president of Ohio's Capital University. Preus pointed out that the seminary in Columbus could be used for preparing Norwegian-American pastors. Five years later the Norwegian Synod decided instead to use the Missouri Synod's Concordia Seminary in St. Louis, chiefly because the Norwegians felt more comfortable with Missouri's theological stance. (There were Norwegian-American seminarians at Capital, however, for one year a generation later: eight students of Anti-Missourian persuasion from the Norwegian Synod's seminary in Madison, Wisconsin, studied at Capital during the 1885-86 school year.)

These churches would also find each other across national lines, of course, in many local communities. Especially as they abandoned their old-country languages and learned to worship in English, a process basically completed by the time of World War II, they found that they had more than the English language in common. In many communities of the Midwest—especially in Illinois, Wisconsin, Iowa, Minnesota, Nebraska, and the Dakotas—the accidents of immigration patterns had brought into being congregations of all three of these ethnic strains.

### *Relationships with Missouri Synod*

Still another common thread for many of the nine groups was a relationship with the Lutherans of the Missouri Synod. With one exception—the Norwegian Synod—the relationship was an unpleasant one. Even the Norwegian Synod's friendship with Missouri had its stormy times; it brought "both grief and joy," as Norwegian-American church historian J. A. Bergh observed decades later.[2] For many of the other groups, the 19th-century relationship with Missouri seemed to be nothing but grief.

Three of the German-background groups were under continuous challenge from Missouri for supposed theological inadequacies. Buffalo battled with Missouri over the doctrine of the church and its ministry. Iowa was actually born as a split from Missouri Synod work in Michigan; the issue was whether differences on some theological points, where biblical and confessional teaching is not decisive, should justify a break in church fellowship (Iowa said they need not). Ohio was a part of the Missouri-led Synodical Conference for almost a decade (1872-81), but left because of differences over the doctrine of predestination.

The Norwegians had less intense involvement with Missouri (language difference provided some buffering), except for the Norwegian Synod. For the most part, the Synod found itself theologically at home with Missouri throughout the 19th century. Yet, even within the Norwegian Synod, there eventually emerged one party which formally defined itself in terms of opposition to Missouri: the Anti-Missourian Brotherhood (1887-90). It is the only organized expression of Lutheranism in the United States ever to *name* itself after what it opposed. The Anti-Missourian faction disagreed with Missouri's position on election and conversion, how human beings are brought to faith. With about a third of the Synod's numbers, they withdrew in 1887 and immediately began to promote interest in a union of Norwegian-American Lutherans who had certain common interests, one of which was antipathy to the emphases of the Missouri Synod.

The Danes of the UELC, it appears, did not directly clash with Missouri. But they did suffer challenges to their orthodoxy from Missouri's friends in the Norwegian Synod, which had doubts about their teaching on justification (see Chapter 7).

### *The Other Germans and the Swedes*

With the other large collection of Lutherans in the United States, those bodies which for the most part found their way into today's Lutheran Church in America, our nine groups had varying relationships.

Ohio was born as a direct offspring of the Pennsylvania German Lutherans. But that familial tie weakened as the 19th century progressed.

For periods in the latter part of the century, Ohio, Iowa, and Texas were associated with many of the eastern, primarily German-origin synods, through the General Council. It brought together several regional synods which were committed to confessional Lutheranism. Ohio and Iowa were present at the organization of the General Council in 1866. Ohio did not join but moved instead into the orbit of Missouri and the Synodical Conference for a decade (1872-81). Iowa also did not fully unite with the Council but maintained a friendly relationship until the Council's termination with the 1917 formation of the United Lutheran Church. Texas was a full member of the General Council from 1869 until its 1895 federation with Iowa.

The Norwegians and Danes had almost no lasting relationship with the eastern German-background groups in the 19th century. But they did connect with the Swedish-origin Augustana Synod, which was concentrated in many of the same Midwest communities as the other Scandinavian immigrants. Some of the Norwegians who became part of the United Norwegian Lutheran Church in 1890 (Chapter 8) had been formally affiliated with Swedish-American Lutherans from the 1850s until 1870.

Again in the 20th century, from 1930 to 1960, the Germans of the former American Lutheran Church, the Norwegians (both Lutheran Free and the Evangelical Lutheran Church), and the Danes of the United Evangelical Lutheran Church found themselves in association with the Swedish-origin Augustana Church in the American Lutheran Conference.

## *Lay Persons Lead*

One of the striking similarities among most of these nine groups is the prominent role played in their early days by lay persons.

*John Stauch* was a licensed lay preacher when he began his work among the scattered German Lutherans living in Ohio. He was not ordained until 1804, when he was 42 years old.

*Captain Heinrich von Rohr*, an officer in the Prussian army who resisted the authorities of his government, was the outstanding leader, after Johannes Grabau, of those who emigrated from Prussia and formed the Buffalo Synod. Von Rohr later became a pastor in the Milwaukee area.

*Hans Nielsen Hauge*, inspiration for the group that gave his name to their synod in the United States, was a lay evangelist in Norway. His problems with the state church and his several years of imprisonment resulted in large part from the fact that he was not ordained.

*Christian Friedrich Spittler*, head of the St. Chrischona mission school in Switzerland, was the father from afar of the Synod in Texas. He remained a lay person all his life.

*Jens Dixen*, a tile digger, exemplified the Danish lay folk in rural communities of the Midwest whose leadership kept the church alive when there were few pastors around.

*Georg Sverdrup* served as a leading theologian among the Norwegian Americans, president of Augsburg Seminary for 31 years, and first leader of the Lutheran Free Church—all without benefit of ordination.

Especially among the Norwegians and Danes, the leadership role of women is noteworthy (see Chapters 5, 7, and 9).

### Questions like Those of Today

These Lutheran churches born in the 19th century had to struggle with many problems: lack of financial resources, absence of trained leadership (both clergy and lay), the search for a fitting Lutheran identity, and always the simple struggle for survival of a frontier people in a strange land. In addition to these problems they faced in common, each seemed to confront a central question uniquely. Those questions may be stated as follows:

- How shall frontier ministry be conducted (Ohio)?
- Who has authority in the church (Buffalo)?
- What is the proper role of lay activity (Hauge's)?
- How can the church be planted in an alien culture (Texas)?
- How shall the faith and human culture interrelate (Norwegian Synod)?
- Can cross-cultural mission be achieved (Iowa)?
- How shall personal faith commitment be nurtured (United Danish)?
- Can the church be unified for mission (United Norwegian)?
- How can congregational freedom be assured (Lutheran Free)?

The most interesting thing about these questions for us today is not their 19th-century settings, though these can be fascinating, but that *they are still with us*. They face us as we seek to be a church in mission today. They face those who are planning a new Lutheran church which will be called to mission as we enter the 21st century.

Three of the questions from our 19th-century origins—those facing Buffalo and Hauge's and Lutheran Free—revolve around *authority in the church*.

Four questions—those of Ohio, Iowa, Texas, and United Norwegian—center on *mission in a new setting*.

The remaining two deal with matters of *faith and culture*. For the Norwegian Synod, it was a quest after the coexistence of faith and human culture. For the United Danish Church, the goal was to see that a surrounding secular culture did not undermine a personal faith commitment.

Not one of these questions has become irrelevant for us who think about the church's identity and task two centuries later. Perhaps reading the stories of how our ancestors in the faith addressed them will help us to struggle with them responsibly and faithfully.

### Religious Conscience and Human Law

One other question that surfaces in a couple of these stories has remained pertinent in 20th-century United States debate: When shall believers decline to obey a governmental requirement in the name of obedience to religious conviction?

Two of the churches whose beginnings are told in these pages have their origin in such a conflict between conscience and civil law. Both Hans Nielsen Hauge (Chapter 3) in Norway and Johannes Grabau (Chapter 2) in Germany spent time in prison for what today would be called civil disobedience.

### From Uniformity to Diversity

The 19th-century origins of these nine churches reveal, finally, the urge to uniformity. The groups were formed around a quest for similarity—in ethnic origin or geographic locale or theological emphasis, and usually all three of these. There was a tendency on the part of each group to think that *its* way of being the church was the only way.

The story of the 20th century, in contrast, has been one of growing acceptance of diversity. As these churches found each other and came together in new church organizations, they were willing to accept a diversity which they could not have endured in one church a century earlier. They accepted—even welcomed—a breadth in geographic spread, in ethnic background, and in theological strains. Without yielding on basic, confessional Lutheranism, they learned that variety in understanding of the church could enrich the whole.

May these nine stories give us new appreciation for the struggles of our predecessors in the faith, help us to understand the questions of our own day, and challenge us to equip ourselves for mission in the years that are coming.

Ohio (1818)

# Trailblazing in the Ohio Wilderness
## How Shall Frontier Ministry Be Conducted?

by Fred W. Meuser and Charles P. Lutz

Ohio, the state, did not exist in 1785. But the river named Ohio was well known in the settled parts of the new United States of America. That was the river which separated the civilized, organized East from the western wilderness.

"Ohio country" was the beginning of the West 200 years ago—and the new nation wasn't entirely sure what to do with it. Leave it as Indian territory or turn it into land for settlers? The "Territory Northwest of the River Ohio" (Northwest Territory, as it came to be called) was that vast region bordered by Pennsylvania, the Ohio and Mississippi rivers, and the Great Lakes. Eventually it would be the states of Ohio, Michigan, Indiana, Illinois, and Wisconsin. Theoretically, it was now part of the United States via the 1783 treaty with Great Britain, which recognized that Britain's former colonies had won their war of revolt and had a rightful claim to the Northwest Territory.

But in 1785 it was not at all clear that the weak central government under the Articles of Confederation could exercise authority over the territory. For one thing, several states had colonial charters granting them land all the way west to the Mississippi (some even to the Pacific Ocean!), and they weren't ready to accept federal authority over their claims. For another, the Indians had not agreed to leave—and wanted compensation if they did so. Thirdly, the British may have lost the war and signed a peace treaty, but in fact their military still occupied forts at Sandusky, Detroit, and points north (they did not finally leave until 1794).

The young national government 200 years ago knew it had to do *something* about the Ohio country. Once the states were pressured into yielding their claims, the next task was to organize the land for sale to settlers. In the Northwest Ordinance of 1785, the Continental Congress set the pattern for land survey which would hold for the entire West. It provided that, from the point where the Ohio River flows out of Pennsylvania, a series of base lines (east-west) and range lines (north-south), six miles apart, should divide the region into townships of 36 square miles each. A square mile would be one section. Each township would have 36 sections, and one of them would be dedicated to the support of public education. Settlers would be able to buy land for $1 per acre.

Next, in the Northwest Ordinance of 1787, Congress provided for the area's governance, from wilderness to territory to statehood (a region could apply for admission to the Union once it had 60,000 people). The area should be free of slavery and its people should have all the rights of the original states. The Ordinances of 1785 and 1787 formed the basis for organizing the rest of the Union to its present character. Daniel Webster later said of the 1787 Act: ''No single law of any lawgiver, ancient or modern, has produced effects of more distinct, marked, and lasting character than this document.''

The first settlements in Ohio country followed soon after—at Marietta in 1788 and Cincinnati in 1789. Indians continued to be troublesome to white settlement for some years, but by 1795 their resistance had ceased. Ohio was open and ready for settling and the people came, enough so that by 1803 Ohio could become the 17th state in the Union. Among those early Ohioans were many

German Lutherans; one who came to serve them was a lay preacher named John Stauch.

## *"The Thought that I Must Preach"*

Born Johannes Stauch in 1762, this man was the pioneer leader of the first organized Lutheran church body west of the Alleghenies, formed in 1818. It later became known as the Evangelical Lutheran Joint Synod of Ohio and Adjacent States, "Joint Synod" for short.

Stauch's parents emigrated from different parts of Germany in 1740, his mother from Hannover, his father from Württemberg. They settled in York County, Pennsylvania, and were married in 1755. Johannes (John) was born there January 25, 1762. He later wrote that his parents were "poor but pious" and that his mother taught the children prayers and Bible verses and exercised strict discipline.

In his autobiography Stauch writes that his childhood was troubled, "until I reached my 19th year."[1] At that point "the thought that I must preach the Gospel took hold upon my mind." He shared his sense of call with his parents, who were supportive, and with his pastor, who advised him to wait and see if the call were the real thing.

While waiting, Stauch became an indentured apprentice in the wagon-making trade in York, then went as a journeyman to Hagerstown, Maryland. There he met and married Elizabeth Haguemire. In the summer of 1787, at age 25, Stauch and his new bride set out for the West, to make their home in the land across the Alleghenies. They stopped in the area just beyond Maryland's western border, called the Virginia Glades (near the present town of Aurora, West Virginia; the western part of Virginia did not become a separate state until 1863).

When they arrived, Stauch writes, the young couple knew of no settlers nearer than 20 miles. But within a year six more

John Stauch
1762-1845

Certificate for a Baptism performed by John Stauch in Washington County, Pennsylvania, on May 30, 1794.

families from the Hagerstown area joined them. The new arrivals brought along a book of sermons and soon John Stauch was designated as the one who should gather them every Sunday for sermon reading, prayers, and hymn singing, which he did, there being no clergy available. When couples began coming to Stauch asking to be married, he sought and received civil authority to perform marriages. But he refused to baptize or to lead in the celebration of Holy Communion, believing that one should be authorized by a properly constituted church structure to administer the sacraments. People were yearning for the ministrations of the church, and Stauch was ready and willing to provide them. But his respect for ecclesiastical order was such that he did not wish to proceed without appropriate authority.

He did, however, agree to continue leading the Sunday meetings for the Aurora settlers and to preach. He desired a preacher's formal training, but did not see how that could be managed, given his family responsibilities:

> The duty of preaching became more impressed on my mind than ever before, and my brethren thought that I could and must preach for them and others. But how could I support a family with a wife and four children in the wilderness, and study for the ministry, was the dilemma. . . . By night I dreamed that multitudes of early settlers would throng the place, tremble and weep at [my] recital of the story of the cross. Sometimes it seemed to me the learned and accomplished in the church would upbraid me for transcending my proper sphere.

At last Stauch resolved not to worry about "the learned and accomplished," at least in terms of his preaching. "I formed a fixed resolution: by the grace of God I would preach Jesus and trust God for good results."

### *"After the Order of Melchizedek"*

Soon he was invited to take his preaching ministry also to Morgantown, to the northwest of Aurora, and then into Fayette

County, Pennsylvania, 20 miles farther north. It was now 1791 and Stauch was becoming essentially a full-time circuit-riding preacher. How his family survived is a mystery, since he received from his preaching rounds only "a meager pittance." But Stauch's passion to carry the Word to "the poor Germans hungering for the bread of life" was so intense that he felt there was no other choice for him:

> My heart sickened within me when I . . . saw the widespread destitution, which has always existed in the Lutheran Church in the West.

He recognized that he went without any ecclesiastical authority, "being of God after the order of Melchizedek."[2] That troubled him somewhat, and he would soon address it, seeking to regularize his status.

When his wife Elizabeth died suddenly in the spring of 1793, Stauch returned with the four children to Hagerstown. While there he arranged to attend the annual meeting of the Pennsylvania Evangelical Lutheran Synod, which convened in late May in Philadelphia. Since it was the only organized Lutheran authority in the Middle Atlantic region, Stauch sought to receive credentials from it for his ministerial work in the West.[3] He was examined by the synod and licensed as a catechist for a period of one year. With that credential, and leaving his motherless children with kin in Hagerstown, Stauch moved west again. This time he settled on farm land belonging to St. Jacob Church, near present-day Masontown, Pennsylvania.

In June 1794 it was back to synod meeting, in Reading, where Stauch was again examined, this time being "found qualified to receive a candidate's license to preach for one year, in Salem, Morgantown, Redstone . . . and still farther West." From his base in Fayette County, Pennsylvania, he organized and served 10 preaching places in German Lutheran settlements—in southwest Pennsylvania and western Virginia, including the flock at

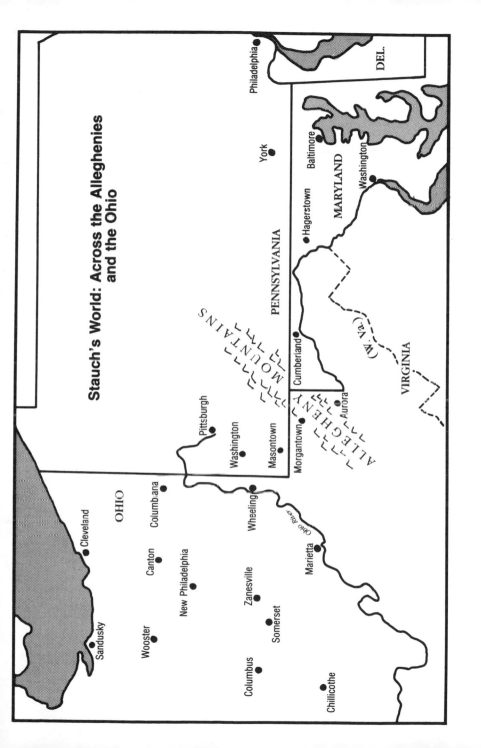

Stauch's World: Across the Alleghenies and the Ohio

Aurora where he had first settled in 1787. Of his time between 1793 and 1796, Stauch wrote:

> I lived, when at home, in a cabin three years and one-half entirely alone, no living creature about me but my horse. My kind neighbors did my washing and baking of bread.

His solitary existence ended in 1796, when he married Catherine Troutman. Then he brought his four children from Maryland to live with him again, ''and continued traveling as extensively as before.'' He tried to make the rounds of his ten preaching points at least once every four weeks. It was an uncomfortable and often perilous existence, traveling on horseback in wilderness, often sleeping under open skies. Stauch was able to write about those days with a note of humor:

> Not infrequently the night found me in the woods, a long distance from any habitation. My only alternative was to tie my horse to a sapling for safe keeping, take my saddle and blanket for a bed and, like Jacob of old, who took a stone for a pillow, lie down in that place to sleep; so I would resign myself to the mercy of the night. And, like him, in the morning I would be refreshed and encouraged by visions of the night, if not like him to see the ladder and angelic visions. For any of us would be willing to take up with Jacob's pillow if we might but have Jacob's dreams.

### Whiskey and Unrest

The political times were also unsettled. The federal government had grown stronger, the 13 original states having agreed to replace the Articles of Confederation with a new Constitution. It was ratified and took effect in 1788 with the election of the first president and a Congress. But there were rumblings of discontent in western Pennsylvania in the early 90s, when a large number of farmers challenged the authority of the central government.

The new federal government needed to raise money for the national treasury. In 1791, one of the taxes it levied was an excise on distilled liquors. Now the German and Scotch-Irish farmers across the Alleghenies in Pennsylvania had found that the most economical way to get the manufactured necessities of life from the East was to distill their grain into whiskey and send it over the mountains in five-gallon kegs on pack horses. When the federals put a heavy tax on their distilled grain, the farmers found a large part of their purchasing power was gone, and with it a convenient way of getting goods from the East. The farmers' distress led to the infamous Whiskey Rebellion of 1794. This was not nonviolent civil disobedience but an armed uprising in which the farmers attacked federal revenue officers who tried to collect the tax, tarring and feathering them, burning their homes, and generally defying the authority of the national government. President Washington sent a 13,000-man army to occupy the western counties, restore order, and enforce the law. No lives were lost and the opposition soon melted away. Stauch does not comment on the rebellion in his autobiography, though it affected the farmers he was serving. But the historian of Pittsburgh Synod Lutheranism offers this comment:

> The Germans were less concerned in actual rebellion against the government than their Scotch-Irish neighbors. The insurrection, however, contributed much to the German population of this part of the country, for in the army sent into Washington County to crush the rebellion were many Germans from Maryland and eastern Pennsylvania, who were so favorably impressed by the country west of the mountains that they resolved to make it their future home.[4]

Meanwhile, across the Ohio River, the situation was starting to look attractive to settlers as well. The Treaty of Greenville (1795) ended the Indian wars on the Ohio frontier and brought security for settlement. The U.S. at last had actual jurisdiction over land it had nominally owned since 1783. A steady stream of new residents now came—from New England and New York, Pennsylvania and Maryland, Virginia, up from Kentucky, and directly from Europe, especially Germany. Civil government for Ohio as a territory was achieved in 1799, and by 1803 statehood was a fact. The capital, established at Chillicothe, moved to Zanesville from 1810 to 1812, then returned to Chillicothe for a few years before permanently locating in the new town of Columbus in 1816.

Ohio, as the century was turning, was "nearly an impenetrable forest," Stauch wrote. Estimates are that trees covered 90% of the state's area. They were so large and so thick that daylight seldom reached the ground. Settlers moved through and lived under this solid green canopy at all times, except where they had cleared the gigantic stands of oak, maple, hickory, chestnut, beech, and buckeye. In those first years the only visible signs of habitation were wisps of smoke rising here and there through the leafy umbrella.[5]

The first generation of settlers simply disappeared from view once they crossed the river. Roads were nonexistent; there were animal and Indian trails but nothing to accommodate carts and wagons. The great National Road, which eventually would cross Ohio roughly along the route of today's U.S. 40 and I-70, in 1806 began working its way west from Cumberland, Maryland. But it would not reach the river at Wheeling until 1818, Columbus until 1833, the Indiana line until 1837.

The forests of Ohio covered soil that was quite fertile for farming. But they had to be cleared. The darkness, the inability to see sky or broad vistas of landscape, the omnipresence of trees to be removed so that a living could be made from the earth— all contributed to a feeling of isolation, depression, and a yearning for other human beings in early Ohio. Many of these pioneers also longed for the ministrations of the church, which had been left behind and, in any organized expression, did not immediately follow them across the Ohio River.

## *Stauch Hears Another Call*

John Stauch knew there was need in Ohio. Many of the first settlers, he wrote, were "pious Germans from beyond the waters and the eastern states." He was able to imagine them as they

> . . . continued in their daily devotions morning and evening in their cabins, kneeling in the dust upon their earthen floors, prayed fervently to the Great Shepherd to send them spiritual guides, to visit their families, baptize their babes, catechize and confirm their children, visit them in their afflictions, speak comfortable words of promise to them in their dying moments and perform burial services at their graves. I heard their Macedonian call for help.

And so Stauch began traveling into the newly opened land of Ohio. It is not clear exactly when these trips began, but he was apparently making them by the year 1800. He would leave his base in Fayette County, Pennsylvania, and conduct a horseback foray lasting several weeks into the eastern Ohio counties due west and somewhat to the north.

Stauch was still under the authority of the Pennsylvania Ministerium and he routinely returned to be relicensed at its annual synod meetings in the eastern part of the state. At last, in 1804, he was "examined and ordained to preach the gospel of reconciliation." Thus ended 10 years of service as a licensed lay preacher, and 24 years of waiting to see if that call he sensed in his 19th year was genuine. John Stauch, who never had formal theological training or *any* formal education beyond the basic schooling he received as a child in York, who educated himself in the Scriptures and the church's theology, was a full-fledged pastor at last.

Two years later, in 1806, Stauch decided it was time to move to Ohio. He resigned his pastorate in Fayette County, where he had been residing for 13 years, and moved with his family to Columbiana County, just north and west of the point where the Ohio River crosses the border from Pennsylvania. He believed that he was the first Lutheran pastor to assume permanent residence in Ohio, and historians seem to agree.

Stauch reports that the first Lutheran community to be organized in Ohio was in Jefferson County (Steubenville area) in 1800. It was one of the settlements he visited on his circuit. In the years between 1806 and 1812 Stauch organized congregations in Columbiana, Jefferson, Warren, and Stark counties in Ohio, and in the western Pennsylvania counties of Beaver and Mercer.

The Pennsylvania Ministerium tried to offer modest assistance. Beginning in 1804 it sent pastors during the summer months into the Ohio frontier. In this way many small congregations were begun, well before there were settled pastors available to serve them. Stauch was the first permanent pastor but he speaks of others who arrived shortly after he did. Churches were organized and served by these men between 1806 and 1812 southwest of Zanesville (Somerset, New Redington, and Thornville).

The Ohio work had a loose tie to the Pennsylvania Ministerium, but increasingly the Ohioans felt isolated from Lutherans east of the mountains. The Ministerium authorized creation of a western conference as early as 1801, but nothing happened for another decade. Then, on October 17, 1812, in Washington County, Pennsylvania, eight pastors and three laymen organized a special conference of the Ministerium, the first Lutheran regional body to be formed west of the Alleghenies. John Stauch of Columbiana County, Ohio, was elected president.

Stauch reports that a number of urgent requests for pastoral services from various parts of Ohio were considered,

but the principal business transacted was to offer up one of those
soul-stirring, heart-edifying, and fervent prayers which seemed to
penetrate the holy heavens and would . . . take no denial until the
Great Shepherd would send able and efficient pastors to supply the
lamentable destitution that prevailed in every direction.

## Next, a Synod in Ohio

The western conference met regularly thereafter, at least annually. The spirit of separateness and independence grew. In 1816
the conference voted unanimously to ask the Pennsylvania Ministerium for permission to organize a ministerium of its own which
could license and ordain pastors and raise funds for its own work.
Stauch and one other representative went to present the request
the next year; it was not granted, but the Ohioans were not de-
terred. In September of 1817 they met in New Philadelphia, Ohio,
to take first steps toward a general conference of Lutherans in
that state. The next year, September 14, 1818, ten pastors, two
applicants for lay ministry licenses, and eight lay delegates met
at Somerset, Ohio, to organize the General Conference of the
Evangelical Lutheran Preachers in the State of Ohio. It was reported that another seven pastors were unable to be present. John
Stauch was elected president.

The new body adopted the constitution of the Pennsylvania
Ministerium with only one change: the name on the title page. It
ordained three candidates for the ministry at its first meeting.

Cordial relations continued between the synod in Ohio and the
Pennsylvania Ministerium. Doctrinally, the Ohio group resem-
bled its parent, which was an outgrowth of the Halle School in
Germany. Halle's emphasis, while Lutheran, was chiefly on piety
and missionary outreach rather than on doctrinal purity. The chief
interest of early Ohio Synod leaders, thus, was the mammoth
challenge of taking the church's ministry to the scattered German

settlers in the newly opened Northwest Territory, not the preservation of confessional Lutheranism. It was not until the middle decades of the 19th century, when a wave of more conservative Lutherans arrived from Germany, that the Ohio Synod became self-conscious about a more confessionally Lutheran stance.[6]

John Stauch shared the pietist emphasis of the 18th-century Halle School in Germany—it was the brand of Lutheran Christianity he was taught. His chief passion in life was clearly the preaching of the word of salvation to people. In the area of Christian behavior, Stauch also stood within the pietist tradition. He was greatly troubled by the laxity of Lutherans and others on the frontier who took part in dancing, or showed disrespect for the Sabbath by making formal visits and "even working in harvest, traveling, hunting and fishing" on that day. He also raised his voice regularly against alcoholic drink:

> I preached that the only safe way was to refrain from it entirely. I taught them to believe, if they would abstain from the use of exhilarating drinks, that they might be sure they would never be drunk, but without total abstinence it was extremely doubtful. But I met with strong opposition from many of my Lutheran members by opposing and condemning these immoral practices.

The conference formed in Ohio in 1818 met annually in its early years. Each year it had an election for president. Stauch was chosen six times during the first dozen years, an indication of the regard in which he was held.

At the 1825 meeting the conference began using the name "Evangelical Lutheran Synod of Ohio and Adjacent States." In 1831 it formed two districts, eastern and western, and the word "Joint" was then inserted before the word "Synod" to refer to the full entity. From that time until its entry into the American Lutheran Church almost a century later (1930) it was popularly known as the Joint Synod.

### Stauch's Later Years

John Stauch continued to live in Columbiana County, serving congregations from that base, until his retirement in 1829. He was then 67 years old and had been serving as a preacher (lay or ordained) for more than 40 years. He explains in his autobiography why he believed it was time for him to leave active ministry:

> I . . . was greatly changed in body, but not in soul, for my soul was changed in my youth, long before I crossed the winter mountains. . . . My stentorious voice, that had been my faithful servant for many years, began to fail in both speaking and singing. I knew this to be a sure presage of my speedy dissolution, and resigned my pastorate. . . .

He moved to Crawford County, Ohio, near Bucyrus, "intending to spend the remainder of my days in quiet retirement, which is so much coveted by old age, and to meditate on the bright and eternal future."

But he was not allowed to spend all his time in quiet meditation. He was pressed into preaching by a fellow pastor in Crawford County. He also threw in his lot with the English District of the Ohio Synod when it was formed in 1836 by a group of congregations wishing to use English exclusively. It was to be a district that would remain fully in fellowship with the Joint Synod of Ohio, but by 1840 ten of its pastors decided to secede, forming the English Lutheran Synod of Ohio.[7]

It is somewhat ironic, and even maybe prophetic, that Stauch, who had always done most of his own preaching and writing in German, felt comfortable with the breakaway group. It resulted from his deep belief that the church needed to become English speaking in order to keep the younger generation and to survive in the United States.

But more than language was at stake. Stauch was deeply disturbed by the Joint Synod's refusal to adopt a strong statement against alcoholic beverages. And as the Joint Synod and its seminary became more self-consciously confessional—over against the influence of the surrounding Protestantism—Stauch believed the so-called ''milder form of Lutheranism'' represented by the English Synod had far greater appeal to frontier people and would spread the gospel more effectively. He grew uncomfortable with the more doctrinally rigid type of Lutheranism which the Joint Synod began to assume in the 1830s and 1840s.

### Two Ohio Lutheran Groups

The Joint Synod of Ohio had opened a seminary in Canton in 1830. It moved to Columbus in 1831 and evolved into Capital University. The seminary component of Capital became one of the parents of today's Trinity Lutheran Seminary in Columbus. Stauch helped the Joint Synod seminary to get started in the 1830s. But he was also part of the group, ten years later, which pulled away to form the English Synod. That group opened its own seminary in Wooster, Ohio, in 1844. When, a year later, the more cautious argued for keeping the school in northeast Ohio, Stauch made the decisive speech favoring its move to Springfield. He reasoned that the future growth of Lutheranism lay to the west and that the school should be where the future lay, not in a place where the present generation felt more safe and comfortable. He remained, at 83, the forward-looking pioneer!

The school was moved to Springfield, where it continues in the form of today's Wittenberg University. Its theological seminary, Hamma School of Theology, was united with the seminary-descendant of the old Joint Synod in 1978 on the Columbus campus, under the name Trinity Lutheran Seminary. Thus, the two schools of theology resulting from the two 19th-century Lutheran emphases in Ohio were reunited after some 135 years. One assumes that John Stauch would have been pleased.[8]

Indeed, from the viewpoint of both the seminary consolidation and the coming union of The American Lutheran Church and the

Lutheran Church in America, Stauch is a significant figure. (The English Synod became part of the United Lutheran Church in America, which entered the Lutheran Church in America in 1963.) John Stauch is claimed by both strands of Ohio Lutheranism. He was clearly not in sympathy with the growing confessional spirit in the Joint Synod. On the other hand, there is no evidence linking him with the so-called Americanized Lutheranism of the kind championed under Samuel Sprecher at Wittenberg University in the middle decades of the 19th century.

In the late 1800s and early 1900s Hamma moved into the Lutheran doctrinal mainstream, paving the way for the consolidation with the Joint Synod's seminary in Columbus decades before it actually occurred. At the same time, the seminary of Capital University in Columbus lost its strongly German character and eventually abandoned its overly rigid Lutheranism, which was the other side of the story.

### *Joint Synod after Stauch*

John Stauch died on July 25, 1845.[9] His wife Catherine lived until Christmas Day of 1848. Ten children were born to them; there were also four from his first marriage. One of those four, Samuel, had as a child been consecrated by his father to the work of the pastoral ministry. "But he chose rather to learn and practice the art of healing the body instead of the soul," John Stauch wrote in his autobiography. It was translated into English by that physician son in 1878.

John and Catherine Stauch were buried at Sulphur Springs, Ohio, a small town near Bucyrus where they lived the last years of their lives.

The Joint Synod extended its work far beyond the borders of Ohio in the century between John Stauch's retirement and the synod's merger into the American Lutheran Church (1930). At merger time it had congregations in 27 states, the District of

Columbia, and five Canadian provinces. It counted 284,000 baptized members, 1034 congregations, and 847 pastors in 1930. It brought into the ALC more people and parishes than the other three partners (Iowa, Texas, and Buffalo Synods) combined.[10]

It is reported[11] that the cemetery in which John and Catherine Stauch are buried was near to a small country road. When Crawford County, early in this century, wished to widen the road, it asked the Lutheran congregation which cared for the cemetery to pay the cost of moving the graves. The congregation declined, with the result that only the headstones were relocated further from the new road. John and Catherine Stauch, plus others, now lie under the widened blacktop.

Perhaps that is not inappropriate. Stauch paved the way for Lutherans and other settlers in this part of the land. Now, as their descendants travel that country road in north central Ohio, the wheels of their automobiles pass over the resting place of John Stauch, wilderness preacher, blazer of trails on the Ohio frontier.

Buffalo (1845)

# From a German Jail
## Who Has Authority in the Church?

by Alfred H. Ewald

In the year of the Ohio Synod's founding, a young man was confirmed in the town of Olvenstedt, province of Saxony, Kingdom of Prussia. Johannes Andreas August Grabau, the 14-year-old confirmand, would emerge in less than two decades as the leader of a group of Prussian Lutherans who were in serious conflict with their government. Soon after, they were to emigrate to the United States and form a Lutheran synod called Buffalo. In the next century it would become part of the former American Lutheran Church (1930) and, 30 years later, the present ALC.

Johannes Grabau was born in 1804 to a landowning couple at Olvenstedt, near Magdeburg.[1] Johannes Andreas Grabau and Anna Dorthea (nee Jericho) brought him, when he was one week old, to St. Laurentius Church in Olvenstedt for Baptism. St. Laurentius was a united (Reformed and Lutheran) congregation served by Pastor H. L. S. Walther.

This is the story of that young man—Johannes A. A. Grabau— and a government-ordained church union which he and his followers could not accept. Grabau was deeply troubled by the pretense that Lutheran and Reformed teaching were the same when they were not. As a result of his resistance to the Prussian government, he was forbidden to officiate as a Lutheran pastor and was imprisoned for more than a year. When offered release from jail, it was on condition that he leave his homeland. Grabau did so, taking five shiploads of fellow believers with him.

### Grabau's Childhood

Johannes's parents were people of deep Lutheran piety. They read the Scriptures regularly in their home and led their two children, Johannes and Lisette, a younger daughter, in daily family prayers.

When Johannes was five, he was enrolled in the parish boys' school at Olvenstedt. The instruction Grabau received was a mixture of Reformed and Lutheran teaching. He later recalled that Pastor Walther took pains to belittle Martin Luther's teachings and to point to the Swiss reformer, Ulrich Zwingli, as the one to follow.

By the time Grabau was 13 and in the midst of confirmation instruction, in 1817, King Friedrich Wilhelm III of Prussia decreed that there should be one Protestant church in Prussia. Lutheran and Reformed churches in Prussia had been in rivalry and strife over the three centuries since the Reformation, and Friedrich Wilhelm wanted to end the rivalry as a way of celebrating the 300th anniversary of the Reformation in 1817. Instead, his creation of the Union Church in Prussia produced strong protests from many of the Lutherans.

### The Prussian Union Church

Friedrich Wilhelm sought the neatness of a single Protestant church structure. The Protestant churches of Prussia were supported by tax money collected by the government. So were the churches' schools. Was the state supposed to permit and pay for two varieties of teaching, and two orders of public worship? The king thought that freedom in such matters would produce intolerable confusion and disorder. So he ordered that a single church be formed.

The Union Church had pastors of both Reformed and Lutheran leaning, of course, and individual congregations tended to follow the orientation of each pastor. What became troublesome was a communion liturgy which all churches were expected to use. It tried to resolve one doctrinal dispute between the Reformed and Lutheran traditions by requiring these words to be spoken at the distribution of the Lord's Supper: "Jesus Christ says, 'This is my body.' " The strict Lutherans, whose teaching was contained in their own communion formula—"Take, eat, this is the true body of our Lord Jesus Christ"—were unalterably opposed to the government-approved wording. From 1831 onward, the king insisted that pastors who refused to use the official language at Communion would be guilty of flagrant disobedience to their king.[2]

Meanwhile, young Johannes Grabau was continuing his schooling. In the fall of 1818 he enrolled in the cathedral school (high school and early college years) in Magdeburg. When his father died in 1822, Grabau found that family finances would make it difficult for him to continue in school. His mother felt he should leave. But Grabau did not quit. He made his way each day, probably walking, from his home in Olvenstedt to Magdeburg, instead of taking a room in the city at the school. He stayed in the classroom at noon to eat his bread.

One day Mr. Wiggert, the teacher, returned to the classroom during lunch break and discovered Grabau eating his meager lunch. Wiggert inquired about Grabau's circumstances and expressed concern. About six weeks later the rector of the school informed Grabau that he had been awarded a stipend of $25 per half year, because of his poverty. Grabau's mother interpreted this to be a divine indication that Johannes should stay in school.

The following year Grabau was commended to the local banker, a Mr. Nitze, as a live-in tutor for his son; the arrangement gave

Grabau a place to live and a way of financing his education. He also served as tutor for the family of a local physician, Dr. Niemeyer.

## Teacher and Pastor

Grabau enrolled at the University of Halle in the fall of 1825, studying chiefly in philosophy and theology. During his studies he wrote a theological essay for which he won a prize of $35. When he passed his final examination with distinction in 1829, the university preacher and codirector of the Royal Theological Seminary at Halle said of him: "His solid understanding of the Holy Scriptures, aptitude, able presentation and development of concepts, edification of thought, and strength of language, joined with a gratifying thoroughness of knowledge and uprightness, indicate that he will serve pre-eminently in his chosen calling, the Gospel ministry."

Grabau first served as a school teacher upon graduation from the university. He taught at the high school for girls in Magdeburg. In August 1832 he became rector of the city school at Sachsa.

Already in February 1832 Grabau had passed his examination for admission to the pastoral ministry, but it was not until January 1834 that he was considered by a congregation. St. Andreas Church in Erfurt had a pastoral vacancy and the magistrate of the city of Erfurt invited Grabau, along with two others, to preach trial sermons. Grabau was assigned to preach on John 12:23. He did so on February 16, and on March 3 was elected as pastor of St. Andreas. He was ordained on June 17, 1834, and installed as pastor in Erfurt on June 22.

A year later, in July 1834, Grabau married Christiane Sophie (nee Burggraf).

## Conscience and Conflict

Grabau's vigorous and scriptural preaching at St. Andreas was blessed with increased membership and attendance; people in

Erfurt were ready to respond to an earnest and decisive Christianity. But Grabau grew more and more uncomfortable with the Prussian Union's suppression of Lutheran teaching. The more he studied the Scriptures and the more he learned of the Union Church's blurring of Lutheran teaching, the heavier it rested on Grabau's conscience to speak out. He objected particularly to the required use of the Reformed liturgy, the orders to be followed for the various services of the church.

Grabau in 1836 made a public declaration that he could not in good conscience submit to the agenda (liturgy) of the Prussian Union, since it accommodated Reformed teachings and opposed the confessions of the Lutheran church and his own ordination vows. Bishop Draeseke of the Thuringia Synod had observed already in 1835: "Grabau's sermons are full of truth and life, but they are too Lutheran." Now the bishop had to respond to Grabau's public statement. He had the consistory advisor, Pastor Moeller, ask Grabau in writing: "Do you, as is voiced publicly, allow yourself any deviation from the prescribed form for any pastoral act?"

The same day, August 30, 1836, Grabau wrote his reply, saying he did indeed deviate, that he respectfully and sincerely asked not to be forced to use the Prussian Union agenda, and that his congregation agreed with him.

Within a week, Advisor Moeller fired off a longer letter. This time he wanted to know whether Grabau:

1. Observed to the letter the Prussian Union church order for all pastoral acts;

2. Ever used a prayer other than the one prescribed in the "united" agenda;

3. Had been authorized by anyone to read the confession of sins after the sermon;

4. Would state what he meant by "congregation";

5. Believed that the congregation had the right to change regulations ordered by the Prussian church;

6. Understood that if individual congregations could make such changes the whole regional church could be split into factions going in different directions;

7. Had instructed his congregation concerning the defectiveness of the prescribed liturgical forms;

8. Would explain how his congregation had reached unanimity on the liturgical changes he favored.

### Grabau's Defense

The reply sent by Grabau contained the following points:

1. He could not use the prescribed form of the Prussian Union agenda in administering the Lord's Supper because it did not express the faith of the Lutheran church as expressed in its confessional books, which are in agreement with the Holy Scriptures. Those books are therefore a higher authority than the Berlin agenda (another name for the Prussian Union orders).

2. He could not use the Union agenda prescribed for Holy Baptism because the Lutheran faith concerning Baptism is mutilated thereby.

3. Nor could he use the prescribed form for burial because the faith worked by the power of God in the redeeming death of Jesus and his glorious resurrection is weakened by the prayers in the Union agenda.

4. He would have to hold to the old Lutheran agenda in regard to the marriage formula because the marriage vows in the Union agenda do not conform to Matt. 5:37; a simple "I do" or "Yes" is enough.

5. He had not used any prayer other than the one prescribed in the Union liturgy but he felt it badly needed changing. He had to insist that the congregation has a right to place the prayer after the sermon, and that the proper place for the confession of sin and absolution was after the sermon.

6. The congregation is not an accumulation of ignorant people who should be allowed no judgment based on Holy Scriptures in

the matter of their own divine worship. The apostle Paul exhorts the congregation at Thessalonica not to quench the Spirit but to test all things. We should not yield to the enemies in regard to matters on which congregations should have freedom, as the apostle writes in Gal. 5:1, "Stand fast therefore in the liberty wherewith Christ has made us free, and be not entangled again in the yoke of bondage." And in 2 Cor. 6:14 we are told that we should "be not unequally yoked with unbelievers." Also, referring to the Smalcald Articles, without the Word of God no congregation can have any judgment in matters of divine services, but with the Word of God the congregation should exercise judgment and have the right to throw off false orders of service and to confess the right.

7. The congregation had been instructed in an address after the sermon which set forth the differences between the Union agenda and the statements of Holy Scripture, without any spirit of accusation of heresy. He had a congregation not given to pretense but rather a Christian congregation which agreed fully with everything he stood for, based on the clear Word of God.

Finally, Grabau wrote, it was a heavy assignment in his whole ministry to promote one faith, as he had vowed to do at his installation, when a different faith based on statutes of men is prescribed in the Union agenda. The Lord said it clearly when he said that no one could serve two masters. He concluded by writing:

> It is becoming difficult to combine certainty of faith and will with humility so that no evil may be mixed with it. But where the statutes or regulations of men are recognized as such and one's conscience before God will not allow obedience to such statutes, every outward force is an unfit means to enforce obedience. I cannot therefore in this instance carry out the assignment given me. I will continue to conduct services according to the order and manner used to this time, but regarding the sacraments and other acts I will use the old agenda to which . . . my congregation has expressed its allegiance.

### *Suspension by Government Officials*

By the fall of 1836, Grabau took his case before the congregation. On the 15th Sunday after Trinity, following the sermon, he explained to his congregation where he stood. He told them that at the time of his installation two years before he was not fully acquainted with the new forms, but that since then he had become completely convinced that he could not use the Union agenda because it did not truly confess the faith of the Scriptures. He would use the old orders which had been developed in Luther's time and which the Andreas parish had confessed since the time of the Augsburg Confession (1530).

Grabau asked the members of his congregation whether they could in good conscience stand with him in this matter. They should give serious consideration to this question and give him their reply in writing as soon as possible. He cautioned them not to be hasty or premature in passing judgment on other congregations and persons who decided to continue with the new agenda, and not to decide in his favor on the basis of personal love for him. It was a matter not lightly to be considered. He wished them the enlightenment of the Holy Spirit in their deliberation.

The lines had been drawn and the matter had grown beyond oral debate. The immediate effect was that Grabau was suspended from his pastoral office by royal government officials. The news spread rapidly and church people in Silesia, Thuringia, and Saxony began to take sides.

The following Sunday, the Andreas church was surrounded by both royal constabulary and local police. Grabau was forbidden to use the pulpit or even to enter the church. A representative of the consistory entered the pulpit and announced the suspension of the pastor.

Following the service, the members of St. Andreas went to the parsonage and stayed until late that evening, being comforted by Grabau in their distress. For some weeks thereafter the church was empty on Sundays but the parsonage was filled. Soon access to the parsonage was also denied.

A member of the congregation named Fils operated a mill; he made arrangements for the people to meet in a room at the mill. Next, the worshipers were fined for attending services there. They were also fined for not sending their children to the Union Church school.

### Dialog with the Bishop

Bishop Draeseke spent several days trying to persuade Grabau to change his mind. The bishop suggested that Grabau use the Prussian Union agenda and then orally advise his congregation concerning the Lutheran teachings that were omitted. Grabau said that would not be a solution.

Grabau explained that he was uncomfortable in the Prussian Union Church because it had no confession of faith which was generally accepted. Bishop Draeseke said the Holy Scriptures were the church's confession. Grabau answered: the Scriptures are God's confession to us, not our confession to God. The church needs such a confession.

Draeseke argued that the Union Church had its confessions, both Lutheran and United. Grabau replied that it was not possible for one church to have two different confessions.

Draeseke told Grabau that, where the two disagree, he could hold to the Lutheran confession. Grabau said that was impossible when his order of service could not follow a Lutheran liturgical form.

Finally Draeseke defended the king's right to enforce such a union and that Grabau would one day see what misery he was creating for himself.

Grabau left Erfurt and went to Magdeburg, where he found a small group of Lutherans who had separated from the Union Church and were holding services in the home of Heinrich von Rohr, a captain in the Prussian military. Then he returned to Erfurt and submitted his resignation to the consistory. A large portion of St. Andreas Church left with him.

He continued to lead services in the mill. When those services were harassed by the police, the people found ways to assemble in homes at night. The police had orders to seek out those places and stop the services, but many of the police felt ashamed to be engaged in such work. The persecuted congregation grew to more than 70 families, plus about 20 single persons.

Meanwhile, the Andreas congregation had requested either the reinstatement of Grabau or the appointment of another pastor who was a strict Lutheran. If their request was not granted they would, with a few exceptions, join the group served by Grabau.

### Arrest and Jail

There was no reply to the Andreas church's request. Instead, Grabau was ordered to appear at the Erfurt city hall on March 1, 1837, ostensibly for another round of questioning. When Grabau appeared, Mayor Wagner announced that the authorities had ordered his deportation from Erfurt because he had refused to obey the order to cease conducting services according to the Lutheran practice; his removal should occur at once. Grabau said he needed some time to prepare for a journey and to arrange for certain necessities. The mayor then locked the door and said to Grabau, "You may write a note to your wife telling her what you need."

Grabau's wife, when she received the note, hurried with her maid to the city hall. (The maid was the widow Dette, who later became the first housemother of the Martin Luther College and Seminary in Buffalo, New York.) The mayor tried to impress Mrs. Grabau with his courteous manner and words of sympathy. When she asked where they were taking her husband, how he would get there, and how he would be treated, the mayor said Grabau would be taken not far from Erfurt, that he would have a comfortable room, and would suffer no need. In a few days she would hear of the place where her husband would be staying.

Mrs. Grabau had forgotten some of the things her husband had requested, especially items needed for a journey in the cold of the night. Neither she nor her maid was allowed to get them, for fear the congregation would learn what was happening to her husband. She was told not to worry, that everything necessary would be provided. She trusted the mayor but soon discovered that she was being deceived.

As the time for departure drew near Pastor Grabau prayed with his wife, commending her, the congregation, their year-old son, and himself to the protection of the triune God.

After dark, the driver and the vehicle which was to convey Grabau entered the yard of the city hall. Grabau, now a prisoner, was put in the wagon, sheltered only by a light woolen blanket. During the night trip, he became deathly ill, suffering stomach cramps and severe vomiting. They arrived at their destination, Heiligenstadt, the next morning.

The conditions in jail were atrocious: Grabau's cell was damp and filthy, the food was monotonously bad, and his cellmates were abusive. As word of his condition seeped out, more and more people sided with Grabau. The congregation at Erfurt determined to stand fast in its Lutheran convictions.

Then, after months of inhuman treatment, it was reported that Grabau's circumstances were improving. He had been given a cleaner cell and a better bed, and was allowed to take daily walks, accompanied by a guard, outside the prison. The milder treatment was the contribution of the prison inspector, a Saxon who visited Grabau in his cell and received instruction in Lutheran teaching, often late into the night. The inspector became a confessor of the faith and later resigned from the Union church. He allowed Grabau to instruct his children and to preach to the other prisoners.

But Grabau's imprisonment continued. His health worsened and he wrote to the royal officer in charge of Heiligenstadt, asking that he be released from imprisonment. He expressed the wish that God would soon enlighten the government to admit its mistake and cease its persecution of those who held fast to the Lutheran confessions.

### *Freedom—for a While*

Meanwhile, Mrs. Grabau was petitioning the minister of justice in Berlin to free her sick husband. She received a curt reply that her husband on royal orders was to be banished to Munich and that she could accompany him at her own expense.

Then, after six months in prison, Grabau received word that he was to be released, by judgment of the district court. But that decision was reversed until a ruling from a higher court in Erfurt or Berlin could be received. So Grabau stayed in jail. By this time at least 20 Lutheran pastors were either in jail or had been exiled.

An aged guard assigned to accompany Grabau on his daily walks once said to him, "Pastor, it is well known that you sit here being innocent and that as a matter of justice you have been declared free. If I were in your place I would know what to do."

At about this time Captain von Rohr was dismissed from his military office because he had refused to attend the Union church and had his child baptized by a Lutheran pastor. A Friedrich Mueller was another who had been deposed because of his Lutheran teaching. These two undertook the task of freeing Grabau. Mueller visited Grabau and told him von Rohr was at the gate with a wagon, waiting to take him to freedom. Grabau, seeing the plan as God's deliverance, went with the guard outside for his usual walk. Once beyond the gate Grabau said to his guard, "I go today where God wills and you so often have advised me." With that, Grabau jumped on the wagon.

It was late in 1837. For the next nine months, Grabau traveled from place to place in Prussia, usually with von Rohr. Often they were just a jump ahead of the authorities, who continued to pursue them. Grabau reports that he frequently walked the stretch from Magdeburg to Eisleben. Many towns had been posted with

"Wanted" notices and promises of a $50 reward for information leading to Grabau's arrest. On one of his stops in Erfurt, his mother-in-law, who had previously defended the Union Church, sent for him and asked to receive the Lord's Supper. With clarity of mind and the conviction that she was near death, she renounced the Union Church and asked to be forgiven for any wrong she had done. She died the next day.

### Back to Prison

The gates of jail yawned for Grabau again. On September 21, 1838, he was recaptured and returned to Heiligenstadt, where the old inspector welcomed him back.

Grabau took sick again. During the fall months of 1838 he appealed to the royal government in both Erfurt and Berlin asking that he be allowed to emigrate with his family. In November he received word that the Lutheran congregation at Magdeburg wished to emigrate and hoped that he would accompany them as pastor.

At last, on November 26, Grabau was informed by authorities in Berlin that he could emigrate under the following conditions:

1. That he not return to Erfurt or Magdeburg for family consideration or other concerns;

2. That he be accompanied by a policeman from Heiligenstadt directly to Hamburg, the port;

3. That he indicate how he intended to pay the cost of the journey;

4. That he remain in custody of the Hamburg police until the moment he boarded the ship;

5. That the police in Hamburg would arrange passage for him.

Grabau believed the authorities were trying to get him out of the country as if he were a criminal who had lost all his rights, and wanted in the process to separate him from his congregations. He would have no part of that, and he so informed the congregations at Erfurt and Magdeburg.

These congregations turned to the emigration authorities and added the petition that Grabau be allowed to leave with them. The year 1838 ended and the government did nothing to free Grabau. He continued to be laid low by illness. In his diary he referred to the imprisonment of Joseph. But he trusted God and found comfort in being remembered by his loved ones with some gifts on Christmas Eve. It was the second Christmas in a row that he was separated from his family.

On January 18, 1839, he wrote that he believed he would not survive his illness. He asked the government to cancel his incarceration soon because his death seemed imminent. He had a final request—to be permitted to spend his last days with his family and in the care of his loving wife.

On January 25 the government granted Grabau a hearing. These questions were asked: Would he desist from all pastoral functions and did he still want to emigrate as soon as he had regained his health? The answer to both questions was "Yes." But still there was no hint of freedom. His wife and child came from Erfurt to Heiligenstadt, to visit Grabau, under supervision. They spoke of the woe and welfare of the church and encouraged each other to cast their burdens on the Lord, for he cared for them.

On March 12, 1839, Grabau was released from his prison cell. The same day Mrs. Grabau received a letter from King Friedrich Wilhelm III, answering her question whether toleration of the Lutheran church in the Kingdom of Prussia could be expected. The king's reply: The Lutheran church is included in the United church; no Lutheran church outside this Union would be tolerated in his country.

### Emigration to the United States

That answer, received by several congregations, was the basis for the decision to emigrate to the United States. These several congregations united under Grabau's leadership, because no people were allowed to leave Prussia unless they could prove to the government that they were going with a pastor.

On June 28, 1839, the first steamship left Hamburg, followed by two more on the 30th, a fourth on July 12, the fifth and last on July 27. All went to Liverpool, England, where they boarded five sail ships bound for New York. The last ship, bearing Pastor Grabau and his family,[3] arrived in New York September 18.

A small number remained in New York City or Albany, but most of the immigrants continued westward to Buffalo. Some 40 families of Pomeranians, led by Captain von Rohr, settled in the Milwaukee area. Congregations were immediately established in both Buffalo and Milwaukee, as were Christian day schools. The original Buffalo congregation, later to be named Trinity Old Lutheran Church, erected its first house of worship in 1840. That same year a seminary, named for Martin Luther, was opened in Buffalo. Johannes Grabau was simultaneously pastor of the congregation and president of the seminary.

In 1843 these Old Lutherans, as they called themselves, were reinforced by another 1600 Prussians who came seeking religious freedom. Three more pastors came with them. One who went to the Milwaukee area, L. F. E. Krause, on October 18, 1843, at Muskego, Wisconsin, ordained a Dane, C. L. Clausen, to serve among Norwegian immigrants. Clausen had stopped to visit Grabau in Buffalo on his way to the Midwest, and Grabau wrote him a letter of introduction to Krause. Thus were connected three ethnic groups of Lutherans who, 117 years later, would be united in The American Lutheran Church.

### Buffalo Synod Formed

Pastor Grabau decided in 1845 that it was time for the Old Lutherans to form a synod. He called a meeting and on June 25, 1845, in Milwaukee, the four pastors and 18 laymen from the

J. A. A. Grabau
1804-1879

Heinrich von Rohr
1797-1874
Prussian military officer,
Wisconsin pastor

congregations organized the Synod of the Lutheran Church Emigrated from Prussia. Later it came to be known by the nickname it was given from the start, Buffalo Synod. Buffalo experienced healthy growth until 1866. From 10 congregations in 1845 it expanded to 24 two decades later.

But from its beginning, Buffalo was in controversy with another group of German Lutherans. They also had come seeking religious freedom and escape from a forced union of Reformed and Lutheran churches. The founders of this group, also chiefly Saxons from Prussia, emigrated in 1838 and settled primarily in Missouri. By 1847 they had organized what is known today as the Lutheran Church–Missouri Synod.

With origins so similar and with such a harmonious view of the importance of Lutheran confessional theology, Buffalo and Missouri might well have come together in one church. The result was quite different: bitter controversy extending over 20 years.

The differences between Buffalo and Missouri centered around the doctrine of the ministry. Grabau insisted on a high theory of the ordained ministry. That is, God confers the ministerial office upon a candidate, properly trained in the true faith, through the officiating clergy of the church body or synod. Missouri, on the other hand, taught that any local group of believers—a congregation—has the right to elect and call any man as its pastor. Ordination, then, was simply the public recognition of that call; it gave the pastor no special powers over the congregation.

Buffalo Synod pastors and members who became uneasy with Grabau's strict views more and more found a home in the Missouri Synod. And Missouri courted them, often starting competing congregations in the same communities where Buffalo Synod churches were trying to survive. By 1866 the still small Buffalo Synod was itself ready for a split. It broke into three parts. The largest group negotiated with Missouri and was taken into that church. A small number who opposed Grabau's leadership (including his old friend, Pastor Heinrich von Rohr) refused to join Missouri and continued as a separate body. When they finally dissolved in 1877 most of them joined the more conservative Wisconsin Synod. The group that stayed loyal to Grabau was the smallest of the three: four pastors and a handful of congregations.

## Grabau's Contribution

After Grabau died in 1879 the little Buffalo Synod gradually softened its views. The strict, controlling behavior of the synod was modified. By the time Buffalo was ready, 50 years later, to merge into the American Lutheran Church, it had become as congregational in theology and practice as its partner synods, Iowa and Ohio.[4] But it retained its firmly conservative doctrinal stance and its solid allegiance to the Lutheran confessions.

When the former ALC was founded in 1930, Buffalo was by far the smallest of the partners. With just over 10,000 baptized members (51 congregations and 41 pastors), it provided a bare 2% of the uniting church's membership.[5] About half of its congregations were in western New York State, with the rest scattered in Pennsylvania, Michigan, Wisconsin, Minnesota, and Ontario. Some of its early strength around Milwaukee had long before gone over to the Missouri Synod or the Wisconsin Synod.

What did Johannes Grabau and the other founders of Buffalo bring to the American scene? Church historian P. H. Buehring summarizes it like this:

> [They brought] a strict confessionalism, a lofty conception of the Lutheran church, a peculiar theory of church government with a tendency to centralize authority in the general organization rather than in the local congregation, and a decided predilection for the old Lutheran forms of worship and church life.[6]

The little synod called Buffalo was born out of conflict in Germany. Its leader for 40 years was a man who knew conflict all of his adult life, first with government authorities in his native Prussia, then with other Lutherans inside and outside his church body in America. Johannes Grabau always had the courage of his convictions, even if that led to disobedience of human law and a term in jail.

The people who came with him from Prussia—and their heirs—also lived with conflict through most of the next 90 years on this side of the Atlantic. The strife meant they would never become a large Lutheran body.

Yet, Buffalo contributed more than its numerical insignificance would suggest to the 1930 merger with Iowa and Ohio. It brought a strong commitment to confessional Lutheranism and an understanding that the church is more than a collection of autonomous congregations.

3

# Lay Evangelism Builds a Missionary Church
## What Is the Proper Role of Lay Activity?

by Rolf A. Syrdal

Less than a year after the Buffalo Synod was born in Milwaukee, the first organization among Norwegian Lutherans in America had its birth some 60 miles away. The Evangelical Lutheran Church in America (popularly known as Eielsen's Synod) was formed April 13-14, 1846, at Jefferson Prairie, Wisconsin, near today's Clinton in southeastern Rock County. It was the origin of a body which 30 years later would be reorganized under the name "Hauge's Norwegian Evangelical Lutheran Synod in America." Who was this Hauge and why did he have a church named after him in North America?

Hans Nielsen Hauge (1771-1824) was a Norwegian who never set foot on American soil. But many of his followers did. To them was given the unique mission of preserving and spreading Haugean principles in a special way, through proclamation and practice, in a new land and a new age.

### Hans Nielsen Hauge

Hauge "was a lay preacher who left a deeper mark on post-Reformation developments in church life in Norway than any

other man. He was the son of a farmer.''[1] The descriptive phrases
"lay preacher" and "son of a farmer" would brand him, in the
early years of the 19th century, as unlikely material to wield much
influence. But few if any students of Norwegian church history
today would dispute Hauge's towering importance.

He was both a farmer's son and a farmer himself. In those days
the farmer (*bonde*) was supposed to be kept in his place as a
lower-class citizen destined to serve the upper classes. Education
for the farming class was discouraged. Any insistence on individual rights or enterprises beyond the farm was viewed as an
uprising which threatened the accepted order of society.

Hauge was a lay preacher. That was considered presumptuous
by the established clergy. The Conventicle Act adopted by the
Danish government in 1741 (the Danes then ruled Norway)
banned public religious assemblies not conducted by the state
church and its official representatives, in these words:

> It shall, furthermore, be absolutely prohibited for anyone, whether
> a man or woman, married or unmarried, to travel from place to
> place, alone or in company with others, or to hold meetings. Each
> person shall remain in his own particular calling, live quietly,
> support himself honestly, eating his own bread; but people may
> visit each other, in order to help and edify each other. No public
> meetings shall be allowed.[2]

This is the law that was used against Hauge, although "his
entire activity was a call to lay and learned to take their Lutheran
teaching, taught to them in their youth, seriously."[3]

> In the early part of Hauge's ministry, the parish pastor brought the
> district bailiff with him to attend one of his meetings in a country
> home. After the service, the pastor announced that "by the au-
> thority of my holy office . . . I hereby forbid Hans Nielsen Hauge
> to conduct such devotional meetings within my parish." Hauge
> asked the pastor "if he had noted anything in my talk that is contrary
> to the pure teaching." The pastor asked the bailiff to reply. He

said, "The decree of 1741 forbids such godly gatherings, and those who commit such acts shall be expelled from the parish, if necessary, by the aid of the sheriff."[4]

Hauge was also a businessman. He encouraged farmers to improve their farming methods, to use water power for building their own mills, and to use their talents in trades to which they were adapted, that they might improve their economic conditions. He started salt works, paper mills, and a trading company with its own fleet of ships. He also encouraged forestry. Such efforts raised the status of the common people so that eventually they were well represented in parliament, which had traditionally been reserved for persons from the upper class.

### Salt for the Norwegians

Hauge was confirmed in 1787 at the age of 16. He took his confirmation seriously, but labored under a sense of sin and guilt that he could not overcome. He read the Bible and Luther's writings, seeking peace. It was not until 1796 that he came to assurance of full forgiveness of sin through God's grace. With this assurance he felt responsible for sharing his joy with others. For the next eight years he sought to bring others to that same personal faith, first in his home community of Tune, in Sogn, later throughout most of Norway and into Denmark as well.

He was successful. Large numbers of people came to his meetings and were converted to a living faith in Christ. The official clergy, many of whom were influenced by a science-based rationalism, were distressed by Hauge's activity. So were the entrenched business interests, since Hauge's revival was producing a social awakening that challenged a Norwegian order in which great privileges were granted to the few.

During the eight years from 1796 to 1804 Hauge was arrested 10 times, but always released after a hearing or a short period in

Hans Nielsen Hauge
1771-1824

prison. The 11th arrest, October 1804, was more serious. Brought
to Christiania (Oslo) in chains, Hauge was put in solitary con-
finement, denied bail, and forbidden all reading and writing ma-
terials. The books he had written were impounded by the
government; a house-to-house search throughout Norway was
made, with dire threats to any who did not turn them over to
authorities.

The zeal with which Hauge was prosecuted indicates the threat
he must have been. He was accused of many things: illegal lay
activity, arousing the lower classes, abusing the freedom of the
press, building a financial organization at the expense of his followers, illegal trade, and more. Intensive searching by state-ap-
pointed agents throughout Norway sought to establish a solid case
against him. His hearing was not held until October 11, 1811,
seven years after the arrest.

Meanwhile Hauge remained under indictment. After the first
two years in prison his condition was slightly improved. Then,
in January 1809, through Count Moltke, he was asked to build
some salt works for the government, since an English blockade

considered the only one in the country capable of this task. He was glad to serve. Later that year he was called back to prison, but from then on his conditions were greatly relaxed. Upon Hauge's return to prison, Moltke gave this testimonial to Hauge's prosecutors:

> The government Commissariat has no one more efficient, more upright, more trustworthy and self-sacrificing than Hans Nielsen Hauge among its commissaries. I ask you, good sirs, to make note of this. And I will add something on my own account: The followers of Hans Nielsen Hauge are among the best citizens. I no doubt am not wrong when I describe them as the salt that will keep the Norwegian people clean and wholesome in the great trials that the present and future times will bring to our land.[5]

When the chief prosecutor sarcastically called him the best witness that Hauge had, Moltke replied:

> In no way! Hauge's activities and the works they bear will be his greatest defense. I do not doubt that he can be convicted on one or another subtle paragraph of law, as interpreted by legal practitioners; but how the Norwegian people and the future will endorse that judgment—that is where I have my doubts.[6]

The statement was prophetic. When all the evidence was in from all areas of Norway, there was no specific accusation that could be used against him except vague applications of the Conventicle Act. Yet, he was sentenced to two years of hard labor in building fortifications. In 1814 the sentence was reduced to a heavy fine and payment of all court costs.

Hauge was now free but his health had been greatly impaired by the years in prison and his property was taken away from him. Because of declining health, he could no longer travel. But the attitude toward him had changed. Bishops and pastors now came to him for counsel. Their support, and the continuing popular acclaim from the common people, brought a change to the Norwegian church that was never lost.

### The Official Church

The Haugean movement developed within a state church that had a degree of official aloofness from the people, with its general tenor established by pastors educated in Denmark. Those describing the church at that time call it a period of orthodoxy stressing formal acceptance of true doctrine, without always calling for a personal relationship of faith in the grace of Jesus Christ or for a new life in him. There was also some preaching of rationalism which undermined faith.

But this picture of the church did not apply to all pastors or to all of Norwegian Christianity.

> The awakening of Haugeanism was not altogether a new life in the Church of Norway. Its root is to be found in the religious life prior to the time of Hauge, especially in orthodoxy, and even more so in pietism. Thus, in common with orthodoxy it strongly emphasized the value of the true doctrine, in accordance with the Word of God and the confessions of the church.[7]

Hauge was a man of the church. He was baptized and confirmed in the church. His confirmation instruction was in Luther's Small Catechism and Pontoppidan's Explanation of the Catechism. With his family he was diligent in attending worship and in receiving the Lord's Supper. An ardent student of the Bible, Hauge was conscious of a burden of sin in his heart until he found peace in the assurance of forgiveness by God's grace.

Soon after his experience of the assurance that God loved him Hauge felt called to share the Word with members of his family and with neighbors. It was the start of his ministry, under the dual compulsion of "faith in obedience" and "deeds of love." Devotional gatherings in homes of friends gradually led him into an itinerant ministry throughout the country. People were hungry for a personal confrontation of the gospel and they thronged to hear him. He also wrote devotional books and tracts and became one of the most widely read authors of Norway.

### Hauge's Theological Orientation

Four points can summarize Hauge's theological emphasis:

1. The Word of God was the source of his faith and the basis of his teaching.

> Hauge [was] filled with an overwhelming faith in the effectual power of the Word. . . . He knew that Word and Spirit belonged together, and that therefore it was always a decisive element of divine power which gave the Word this capacity of breaking through [into the hearts of people]. But he also underscored that the Word was the object of human appropriation through reason, experience and feeling. There must be no "idolatry" regarding the Word. It must be investigated and meditated on in serious reflection. But finally it is still a question of faith and obedience on the part of the people if the Word should truly accomplish that which was its destiny and goal with every individual who heard or read it.[8]

When speaking on Rom. 9:18-21, Hauge comments, "To do good, or to convert ourselves by our own strength, is something we are unable to do. We see that God is the cause of our salvation, and we ourselves are to blame if we cast off salvation."[9]

2. Hauge's preaching was law and gospel. He preached repentance and faith, admonishing people to live by the faith they professed, as given in the doctrinal statements of the Lutheran church. He was true to Luther's explanation of the Third Article, recognizing that it is God who calls the sinner to repentance and who gives power to accept that call and to live the Christian life. Hauge was practical, differing from the pietists he met who seemed to minimize the sinful nature of humanity so that salvation by their own power was made plausible. He also opposed their attempt at a mystical separation from the world. Hauge recognized that Christians are called to live in the world as servants of their Lord. He loved his church, his countrymen, and his homeland, seeking their welfare without separating himself from them. He

did not consider himself a pietist, though earlier pietism had definitely helped to open the way for his person-to-person, group-to-group activity.

3. Hauge always supported the organized church. He attacked preachers who did not preach the Word of God or who neglected their spiritual ministry, but never the church. When he wrote his *Testament to His Friends*, he admonished them to regard the Bible as their dearest treasure. He also reminded them,

> Your friends know that we have not at any point separated us from the Lutheran church up to this time. . . . In all respects you are admonished, hereafter as in the past, not in anything to separate yourselves from the Lutheran church.[10]

4. Hauge carried out his ministry among the common people, as a layman. He never tried to take the place of the pastor, or to assume the pastor's duties. Rather, he wanted to reestablish the ministry of the ordinary believer of apostolic times: the believers "who had been scattered preached the Word wherever they went" (Acts 8:4).

In 1924, 100 years after his death, Hans Nielsen Hauge was officially vindicated and commended by the Department of Church of the Norwegian government. Conceding that its predecessors had prosecuted him, the 1924 government expressed this recognition:

> Hans Nielsen Hauge aroused the greatest awakening that has ever taken place among us, and accomplished the breakthrough of religious freedom in the country. . . . The department would consider it fortunate and fitting if the pastors—starting with the awakening that blossomed forth under Hauge's work—would use the opportunity God gives that a similar, sound country-wide awakening might take place for the welfare and blessing of the Norwegian people.[11]

## Haugeanism in America

Most Norwegians who emigrated to the United States were Lutherans. They brought with them the dual heritage: church and Haugeanism. Their reason for emigration was basically economic. There had been times of depression in Norway—high taxes and meager income from the small farms, many of them with infertile soil. There was a growing population and little opportunity for the landless. The wealthy landowners, the ruling gentry, and others of the upper classes were not smitten with "America Fever." It was the small farmer, the local tradesman, and young people with a bleak future who left for the land of opportunity across the Atlantic.

It was among just such people that Hauge's work had been most effective. His emphasis on a personal commitment to Christ had become part of their heritage. The church also had given them sacred memories. It was in the church that they had been baptized, confirmed, partaken of the Lord's Supper, and learned the hymns they loved. These too were part of their heritage.

But they also inherited the relationship between the church and Haugeanism. There was a barrier between the church with its official attitudes and formal liturgy on the one hand and the Hauge groups with their unofficial status and informal meetings on the other. Gatherings for spiritual fellowship, Bible study, and devotional nurturing were not considered a part of the official church in Norway.

This church/Hauge distinction played a part in the struggle over the kind of church to be created in this country. The problem had a simple answer: forget the situation in Norway and start afresh by uniting all aspects of Christian ministry—formal and informal, pastoral and lay activity—into one church organization, for a vibrant church in free America.

But the problem was not faced. Instead of working to preserve both emphases by welding them together, both sides tried to transplant their systems wholly to the new home, with all the inbred suspicions of each other that existed in Norway. Thus were sunk the roots of a "pro-church" and a "pro-Hauge" group, causing competition and strife instead of cooperation and mutual respect.

## *Enter Elling Eielsen*

Elling Eielsen was the early leader of the Hauge group in the United States. He came by this title honestly, traveling and preaching effectively in the footsteps of Hauge through many parts of Norway and Denmark. While endorsed by Bishop P. O. Bugge of Trondheim and supported by a few pastors, he was opposed by most of the clergy. Eielsen came to America in 1839 and centered his work among Norwegians who were settling in Illinois' Fox River Valley (Kendall and LaSalle counties). Later he worked in southern Wisconsin. He conducted evangelism ministries and organized what he called "scattered fellowship groups." He was preeminently a lay evangelist with deep concern for vital personal faith and life in Christ. But he had no experience in establishing a church.

> If Eielsen had a greater vision of the external organization and had a greater ability to organize people in congregations, he could certainly have gathered a larger synod about him. But that was not Eielsen's strength. If he traveled about preaching conversion and faith, then other pastors followed and organized congregations. . . . The people had to have ministerial services, with sacraments and confirmation instruction. It was natural that they could not receive this from one person and be served by proclamation of another.[12]

Eielsen did, however, take steps in the direction of organized congregations and a church body. He walked to New York to have Luther's Catechism and Pontoppidan's Explanation printed

Elling Eielsen
1804-1883

in Norwegian and English, as basis for training people in the true faith. In 1841 a log house was built under Eielsen's direction in the Fox River settlement; it was the first church of Norwegian Lutherans in America. In 1843 Eielsen was ordained as the first Norwegian-American pastor, on call from the Fox River congregation, by Pastor Francis A. Hoffman of the German-background Michigan Synod.

### Eielsen's Synod

In 1846 Eielsen became one of the organizers and the first president of the initial synodical body among Norwegian Lutherans in America. It was formed at Jefferson Prairie in Rock County, Wisconsin, just north of the Illinois border, on April 13 and 14, and was named "The Evangelical Lutheran Church in America." From the beginning, its popular name was "Eielsen's

Synod.'' Also from the beginning, it was torn by dissension. Three times in its history—1848, 1856, and 1876—groups separated from Eielsen and went their own way. The 1876 break was the largest and took the mainstream of the Hauge movement away from the Eielsen Synod and into a new body to be known as ''Hauge's Synod.''

Meanwhile, pastors were coming from Norway with full theological training and experience in the state church. They placed emphasis on churchly organization and ritual. These became the marks of another Norwegian Lutheran body, ''The Norwegian Evangelical Lutheran Church in America'' or ''The Norwegian Synod,'' as it was popularly known. It was organized in 1853, also in Rock County, Wisconsin, just a few miles west of Jefferson Prairie, in October 1853 (see Chapter 5). The pastors who formed the Norwegian Synod met with people in their homes, as Eielsen did, and doctrinally there was little difference in their constitutions. There was general respect for Hauge and his emphases among Norwegian Synod pastors, as expressed by Pastor A. C. Preus, first president of the Synod:

> When Hauge appeared sixty years ago the Norwegian clergy was for the most part unbelieving and perverted, and the few who could still be accounted as believing pastors were nearly all steeped in pietistic errors. Without trying to determine whether or not Hauge acted in accordance with churchly order, it seems that if Hauge had remained mute the stones would have spoken.[13]

The two synods had some disagreement in areas pertaining to lay activity, but in the spirit of Christ and on the basis of conditions existing in America at the time there could have been a harmonious agreement and possible union between them. But it was not to be. Their differences were increased by the behavior of Pastor Johannes Dietrichson, who came from Norway for two periods to correct what he considered to be gross disorganization of the Norwegian churches in America. ''His definite program was the projection of the Church of Norway as the church of the Norse immigrants to America.''[14]

## Defining Church Membership

There was similarity of doctrinal statements in constitutions prepared for congregations by Dietrichson and Eielsen. But there was a broad difference in rules for membership. Dietrichson demanded that members promise "to submit to the church regulations which the Church of Norway shall establish" and "not to accept or recognize anyone as pastor or spiritual leader who cannot prove that he has been truly called and regularly ordained as a Lutheran pastor according to the Norwegian Church's ritual," and to be obedient to such a called pastor "in all his demands which agree with the fatherland's ritual.''[15]

Eielsen's constitution rejected the "popish authority" of the clergy, declaring further that:

> No one ought to be accepted as a member of our body, except he has passed through a genuine conversion or is on the way to conversion, so he has a noticeable sorrow for his sin, and hunger and thirst after righteousness. . . .[16]

Fortunately, the Norwegian Synod drew up its own constitution, omitting Dietrichson's call for submission to Church of Norway regulations. Fortunately also, there were pastors in the Eielsen Synod who objected to Eielsen's clause concerning membership, insisting that only God could discern the hearts of people.

Pastor Østen Hanson led a call for revision of the Eielsen Synod constitution in 1874. He had served as a member of the synodical council since 1863 and then became president of the synod. The revision eliminated the clause on membership, while preserving an emphasis on the spiritual commitment of members and the importance of lay participation in the work of the church. A new emphasis was placed on building a strong synodical structure on the basis of a common faith.

The revised constitution evinced the basic Lutheran character of the synod. . . . For the sake of peace in the synod the use of Norwegian vestments was not advocated. . . . The synod was composed not only of congregations but of pastors also. A church council with more lay than clergy members was elected to manage affairs between synodical meetings.[17]

This revised constitution was adopted in 1876. It was more than a simple revision, however, and marked the parting of the way with Eielsen, who rejected the changes. He continued his synod under the old name, so the followers of the "new constitution" took the name "Hauge's Norwegian Evangelical Synod in America." (A tiny Eielsen Synod continues to this day; in 1983 it reported two congregations with 50 baptized members and no clergy. Elling Eielsen died in 1883.)

### The Hauge Synod

Based on its "new constitution," the Hauge Synod could continue the work of the synod organized by Eielsen in 1846 without interruption. *Budbaereren* (The Messenger), the Eielsen Synod periodical since 1868, continued as the official organ of the Hauge Synod. The officers of the old synod remained to serve in the new. The basic principles of Haugeanism were unchanged. But the new synod, freed of Eielsen's distrust of churchliness, was actually more representative of true Hauge spirit than the old. It began to grow and develop on the basis of pastors and laity united in common commitment.

At the time of the synodical reorganization Hauge's Synod numbered approximately 7,500 members in fifty-nine congregations served by twenty-four pastors. . . . only a handful remained faithful to Elling Eielsen.[18]

In 1914 it was reported that Eielsen Synod had 1400 members

Østen Hanson
1836-1898

in 27 congregations served by 5 pastors, and the Hauge Synod had nearly 40,000 members in 364 congregations served by 169 pastors.[19]

There were many outstanding pastors and lay leaders in the Hauge Synod, but they do not stand out as lone eagles soaring above the mass. Østen Hanson continued his forceful leadership. Born in Norway in 1836, he emigrated to Minnesota in 1851, where he farmed for several years. Ordained in 1861, he served as a pastor in Goodhue County, Minnesota, from that year until his death in 1898. He served as president of Eielsen/Hauge in 1875-76 and 1887-93. He was also president of the church's foreign mission committee and of the board of its Red Wing Seminary. He was an evangelistic Haugean, but also a man of the church, interested in well-educated clergy and lay workers.

Hanson had promoted a seminary project during the Eielsen Synod years, but all efforts had failed. In 1877, property purchased by the Eielsen Synod in Red Wing, Minnesota, where building was started in 1870, then sold for lack of funds, was again on the market. Interest in building a seminary was stronger than it had been in the Eielsen Synod, and the Red Wing property was purchased with the help of a Hans Sande, who mortgaged his farm to provide the down payment. In a great, united effort it became possible to open Red Wing Seminary and College the following year. Later an academy was established in Jewell, Iowa.

A home for orphans was built in Beresford, South Dakota, followed by a home for the aged. The church expanded through a centralized home mission program, utilizing both pastors and lay people to establish congregations in new geographic areas.

### *Lay Activity Continues*

All this organizational effort did not mean a diminution of spiritual emphasis. A wholesome tension between organization and spirituality existed, each keeping a check on the other.

There was a continued strong emphasis on the individual's relationship with Christ—the grace of God unto salvation and his sustaining grace in Christian living. For the strengthening of the faith, prayer meetings and small group Bible studies were found in every congregation.

Lay activity was encouraged as an active force within the congregation and the synod. Lay people were appointed, for periods of one to three months, to work with pastors in the congregations. At times the lay activity reverted to the old distrust of the clergy, as in Eielsen days. But Østen Hanson had sought to provide pastoral leadership as guidance within the lay movements and this became the norm: pastors and lay people working together to proclaim the gospel and build the church. One of the synod's lay evangelists, Mr. E. L. Skotvold, summed up the synod's understanding of the gospel when he spoke of evangelism at Red Wing Seminary.

Evangelism at Red Wing Seminary did not mean only a pure and correct doctrine subscribed to, but a heart experience of the "Christ in you the hope of glory.'' It meant being orthodox in experience and practice as well as orthodox in doctrine.[20]

The synod supported independent lay organizations within the church, publishing announcements and reports of their meetings. But it encouraged its laity to increased activity within their own congregations, calling them as members to be responsible for congregational welfare and growth. Congregations had the right to call their own pastors and to set their own programs in consultation with the pastor. They also had discretion in the use of the suggested liturgies.

## *Mission to the World*

World mission activity comes in response to a deep spiritual concern for the non-Christian peoples of the world. Such concern was awakened among Lutherans in Europe during the spiritual renewal that came with the pietist movement in the latter quarter of the 17th century. Led by Philipp Spener and August Francke, the movement spread from Halle University in Germany to the North. Two Danish kings, Frederick IV and Frederick VI, were inspired by pietism. Under their sponsorship mission work was started in India (1705) and among the Lapps of northern Norway.

A Norwegian pastor, Hans Egede, in 1721 established a mission among Eskimos in Greenland, which succeeded against great odds. Bishop Bugge, under the influence of the pietist movement, published a mission periodical between 1821 and 1823.

The first Norwegian mission society was started in Stavanger in 1826. Since the state church did not assume leadership in the movement and took no responsibility for sending out missionaries, many small independent mission societies sprang up. An outstanding Haugean on Norway's west coast, John Haugvoldstad, succeeded in uniting these scattered societies into a single organization, the Norwegian Missionary Society, in 1842. The society sent its first missionary, Hans Schreuder, to the Zulus in

Natal, South Africa, in 1843. The same society began work in Madagascar in 1867.

As Norwegians were emigrating to the United States in the latter half of the 1800s, much of this new mission zeal came with them. They were especially interested in the work of the mission societies in Norway and constantly stimulated by reports in their church periodicals on Norwegian mission work in various parts of the world.

Despite the struggles to become established in their new homes, the immigrants continued to exercise their zeal for missions personally by contributing money to mission societies in Norway. As personal contact grew with Norwegian missionaries who visited the churches in America, the interest also grew. Soon came a sense of calling to a more active role in the work through sending missionaries from their own ranks in America. Discussions among various Norwegian-American Lutherans led to a first foreign mission meeting in 1883. At the beginning this new Mission Society sought to stimulate mission zeal but did not function as a sending and supporting agency.

At the 1887 meeting of the Mission Society, Professor Georg Sverdrup of Augsburg College (see Chapter 9) raised the question: "How can mission be a congregational concern for our Norwegian Lutheran congregations?" After discussion, the following conclusion was reported:

> . . . wherever there was a Christian congregation, and where God's Word and the sacraments were given their rightful place, there the mission for the conversion of the non-Christian should be a congregational concern, not only the concern of the individual. Whether the congregation was large or small, poor or rich, old or newly established . . . mission should be common cause for the entire congregation, just as certainly as the support of the pastoral office and the instruction of children in the Christian faith . . . .[21]

## On to China

At first the Norwegian Americans thought in terms of mission outreach through independent societies, as in Norway and other countries. The idea of mission tied specifically to the church (synod) was new, but it would be the next step.

China had opened to Western missionaries and was emerging as the great challenge of the late 19th century. The Norwegian Mission Society had begun work there and some of its missionaries visited the Norwegian Lutherans in America en route to China, stirring a great wave of interest. In 1889 the Mission Society of the synods passed the following resolution:

> The assembly wishes to alert the attention of all Christians to the call that has come from China, especially to the Norwegian church people in America, and to encourage them to also remember the China Mission in their prayers.[22]

A proposal to begin work in China was presented to the 45th annual meeting of the Hauge Synod in Jackson, Minnesota, in 1890. The matter was typically referred to a committee for further consideration.

> A number of those present . . . were dissatisfied with the delay. They gathered around a wagon-box behind the church to discuss matters and take action. There the Norwegian Evangelical Lutheran China Mission Society was formed (June 11, 1890).[23]

In August of that year the first meeting of the China Mission Society, with representatives from both the Hauge Synod and the United Norwegian Lutheran Church (see Chapter 8), was held in Goodhue County, Minnesota. It was decided at once to call Pastor H. N. Ronning and his sister, Thea Ronning, as missionaries to China. Mr. Daniel Nelson, a farmer from Eagle Grove, Iowa, was present. He had already sold his farm and was ready to leave for China, but was not at that time called by the Society. He and his family sailed for China in September 1890 and became the first Lutheran missionaries from America to that country.

At the 1891 meeting of the Hauge Synod, the committee appointed the previous year presented the following resolution:

> We believe and acknowledge that the call that comes to the Norwegian Lutheran church people in this country must be looked upon as a directive from our Lord.
>
> As this call has, in a special way, reached and been noted within the Hauge Synod, we believe that the time has come that our Synod take some serious action in this matter that the Lord has set before us.
>
> Seeking to do God's will, we hereby declare ourselves as a Synod to establish a mission work in China, and to develop the work according to the grace and ability that God will grant us; on the evangelical teachings and confessions.[24]

The resolution was adopted and immediately implemented through calling as missionaries those already called by the Society—the Ronnings—with the addition of Miss Hannah Rorem. They left for China in October of 1891.

There were complications because of the double call to the Ronnings. After negotiations, the Society yielded to the Hauge Synod, which became the sending agency for the Ronnings and Miss Rorem. The United Church then took responsibility for the China Mission Society, which became its synodical mission agency. The United Church extended a call for China service to Pastor and Mrs. Sigvald Netland, Mr. O. S. Nestegaard Jr., and later to Mr. and Mrs. Daniel Nelson as its first missionaries.

By these actions, the concept of world mission was no longer an extra activity of the few, united into independent societies, but became a normal and central function *of the church* in the Hauge Synod. It was quickly followed by the United Norwegian

Church, whick took over the Mission Society and made it their synodical function.

The Hauge Synod action stimulated further actions among the other Norwegian Americans. The United Church and the Lutheran Free Church established their own work in Madagascar. The Norwegian Synod assumed responsibility for work in Zululand and Natal, South Africa, later also starting its own work in China.

### Norwegian-American Unity in China

Norwegian Lutherans in the United States united their work in China when they formed the Norwegian Lutheran Church of America in 1917. The Lutheran United Mission was organized in August of that year with work in the north central China provinces of Honan and Hupeh. From that time until the work was formally discontinued with the departure of the last missionaries in 1950, the China mission was the largest overseas effort conducted by Norwegian-descended Lutherans in the United States. Christian communities continue in China to this day as a result of that work, and visits by Lutherans from America in the past decade have reestablished contact with those communities.

The abiding contribution of Hans Nielsen Hauge shows clearly against the backdrop of the Norwegian state church of his time. There were several theological trends, but by and large the state church was true to confessional Lutheranism, in both teaching and preaching. The latter was done in a highly liturgical setting. Contact between clergy and congregation was official, perfunctory, and aloof. Personal relationship of members with Christ may have been taken for granted, but was not emphasized. Ministry was general, to the group rather than to individuals.

We therefore find differing answers to the spiritual struggles of personal confrontation with law and gospel. Some never moved beyond the burden of guilt. Others found "cheap grace" in a cultish type of revival, without remorse. Still others depended on a nominal acceptance of the church's creeds and the external practice of church rites and regulations. And some simply gave up, leaving the state church for other denominations.

It was at this point that Hauge stepped in. What he brought was something new. As the prophets called erring Israel back to the rock from which they had been hewn, so Hauge called the Norwegians back to the Word of God as patterned in the apostolic church. God, in mercy, seeks the person through the Word. This Word is to be proclaimed by those who are the children of God. It is by the preaching of the law that we recognize our guilt, and therefore our need of grace. It is by the gospel that the word of grace reached the hearts of people to kindle faith. Saved by grace through faith, each person becomes a living stone in the church to serve fellow human beings, to the glory of God. The gospel, personalized, personalizes mission.

# 4

## Texas (1851)

# Planting the Church in an Alien Culture

## How Can Lutheran Identity Be Maintained?

### by Frank R. Wagner and Charles P. Lutz

Germans began arriving in Texas in large numbers about the time Texas arrived in the United States. The former Mexican territory became an independent republic in 1836, then entered the union as the 28th state on December 29, 1845.

Among the Germans flowing into Texas in the 1830s and 1840s were some who sent letters home bemoaning the total absence of pastoral care. That word reached a mission school near Basel in Switzerland. Because of its response, pastors came and the First Evangelical Lutheran Synod in Texas was born on November 10, 1851.

This is the story of how the Lutheran Synod in Texas came to be, through the concern of a faithful layman and a mission institution in Switzerland, neither of which identified as Lutheran.

### *Texas: From Mexico to the United States*

Prior to 1821 Texas was under Spanish rule as a part of its Mexican territory. The first known European settlements in Texas came with Spanish Roman Catholic missions established for the purpose of evangelizing the indigenous people, the Indians of various tribes.

When Mexico gained independence from Spain in 1821 the European colonization of Texas began in a major way. Moses Austin developed an agreement with Mexico under which Americans from various states of the Union could settle in Texas. Many did, especially people from states of the South, who brought along their slaves. Europeans also came directly from England, Ireland, France, Sweden, Norway, and Germany. By 1836, some 25,000 white settlers had arrived.

Mexico, wishing to retain Texas as a province, kept tight control over the settlers, who grew increasingly rebellious. In 1836 they declared Texas an independent republic. After just a few months of battle the Texans were victorious. The new republic was quickly recognized by the United States, England, France, and Belgium. Immigration from Europe and the United States increased significantly. By 1850, 150,000 U.S. white settlers, plus 50,000 black slaves, had moved to Texas. More thousands came from Europe. Among them were large numbers of Germans.

What attracted the Germans? A bad economy at home was the chief reason they left. Overpopulation was a factor. Some of the younger, more educated Germans left because of the feudal political systems and lack of freedoms in their homeland. And some Germans left for Texas out of a spirit of adventure. But the one reason Germans did *not* have for moving to Texas in the 1830s and 1840s, it appears, was religious freedom. In that respect they differed from their compatriots who founded the Buffalo Synod (see Chapter 2) and the Missouri Synod.

The first known German colony in Texas was Industry, in what is today's Austin County, in 1831. Next came Biegel, 20 miles southwest, and in 1834 Cat Spring was settled. Some 100 miles to the southwest, along the lower Guadalupe River in today's

Dewitt and Victoria counties, sprang up another cluster of settlements, including Yorktown, Meyersville, and Victoria. Significant German communities also were developing in the urban centers of Galveston, Houston, Austin, and San Antonio.

All of this settlement was occurring in the decade of the 1830s, during the years just before and just after Texas became an independent republic. In the decade of the 1840s something new came along: societies were forming in Germany to organize and direct immigration to North America. The first such group which chose Texas was the Society for the Protection of German Immigrants in Texas. Because it was backed by 24 dukes and princes, it came to be known as the *Adels-Verein* (Noblemen's Society). Between late 1844 and the spring of 1846, the Society transported 35 shiploads of Germans, totaling close to 5,700 people, to Galveston and thence into various communities of south central Texas.[1]

## *Prince Carl of Solms-Braunfels*

The Noblemen's Society had admirable intentions. Financial speculation and political goals were explicitly ruled out; only philanthropic concerns were to be served. The Society sought to accomplish two objectives: to provide a safe program of travel and settlement in Texas for Germans who were suffering due to deteriorating economic conditions at home; and to relieve some of the pressure of overpopulation for those who remained in Germany by encouraging emigration.

But despite the good intentions, things did not go well. The organizers of the Society were lacking in very basic skills and knowledge necessary for such an undertaking. Their previous experience was primarily in military service and as minor nobility. They had little knowledge of financial planning, purchase of land in a foreign country, the tools and supplies needed for agriculture in Texas, and the disposition of Indians in Texas toward European settlers. As a result, tragic mistakes were made which caused death for hundreds of the immigrants and sickness and suffering for nearly all of them.

The contract between the immigrants and the Society asked each single immigrant to pay 300 gulden (equivalent to about $125) and each family to pay 600 gulden. In return, the Society would provide transportation from Bremen to Galveston, land transport to the colony with wagons and tents furnished, homes built by the Society in the colony, ownership of 160 acres of land per single man or 320 per family, farm and building equipment at minimal cost, and all else that would be needed for the general well-being of the people, such as church, school, hospital, drugstore, and a means of communication. The money remaining would be returned to the people as credit for buying goods from the Society. The agreement looked highly attractive. At least many Germans thought so: nearly 5,700 signed up and made the trip in 35 ships which arrived in Galveston between July 1844 and April 1846.

From the start, problems of miscalculation and mismanagement revealed themselves. The trip to Texas took at least two months. Conditions aboard ship were poor. Food was insufficient and had to be rationed. Sanitation was a major problem. People had to sleep in close quarters, five persons to a room measuring six feet by six feet. The middle decks of the ships were in total darkness and the decks were seldom cleaned. Sickness spread through the people. Many became seriously ill and some died at sea.

Awaiting the arrival of the first 400 in Galveston in 1844 was the Noblemen's Society organizer in Texas, Prince Carl of Solms-Braunfels. (Solms-Braunfels is a region in the German state of Nassau, some 25 miles northwest of Frankfurt.) Prince Carl had not been able to arrange to buy land for a permanent settlement, so he took the Germans, tired, sick, and angry from the ocean voyage, to a temporary settlement at Indianola, near Port Lavaca, southwest of Galveston along the Gulf Coast. They waited there in a tent city until March of 1845. On Good Friday, March 21, some 200 German immigrants finally arrived at their new home, about 100 miles inland along the Guadalupe River. They named it New Braunfels.

Since the directors of the Society had greatly miscalculated expenses and because of the temporary costs Prince Carl accrued in Indianola, he had to borrow heavily. Debts piled up. At last the Society replaced Solms with Baron Ottfried von Meusebach. He was far better qualified, but could not keep the Society from going into bankruptcy. When Meusebach wrote to the Society asking for a minimum of $24,000 to pay off creditors, the Society replied that $24,000 plus another 4,300 immigrants would be arriving shortly.

Meusebach knew that New Braunfels could not support or house 4,300 more people. Somehow he managed to buy another 10,000 acres of land 80 miles northwest of New Braunfels, with plans of sending the new arrivals there. In December of 1845 the 4,300 arrived in Galveston. Meusebach met them and took them to Indianola. They should remain only a short time before moving inland to New Braunfels and beyond, but severe problems arose. In March 1846, 100 wagons which had been contracted to transport the immigrants inland instead went under contract to the United States government. War with Mexico had broken out and the U.S. Army could pay the teamsters a higher price.

Sickness spread through the Indianola camp. Some 300 men, women, and children died there. Through the spring and summer of 1846, the more fortunate ones left the coast as best they could, headed for New Braunfels. The contagion accompanied them and more died along the way.

### Fredericksburg Is Founded

On May 8, the first group of settlers reached the land that Meusebach had purchased 80 miles beyond New Braunfels. They named their settlement Fredericksburg. Before long, it had a thousand inhabitants. Others had started new settlements near New Braunfels. Still others began colonies around Fredericksburg. In total, nearly 5,300 persons docked at Galveston between October 1845 and April 1846. Approximately 1000 of them died before reaching a permanent home. Hundreds more decided to try their luck in the cities of Galveston, Houston, or San Antonio. A few, broken in spirit but not in purse, bought a return passage to Germany. The majority of the almost 5,700 brought by the Noblemen's Society, however, did find their way into one of its settlements.

Meusebach also arranged a peace treaty with Comanche Indians, who occupied land north of Fredericksburg beyond the Llano River. He established two settlements there.

But despite Meusebach's abilities, the Society soon came to an end. It was in extreme debt and when the organizers in Germany learned of the severe conditions of pioneering life in Texas, they decided to end the enterprise.

Life in the settlements was difficult for the immigrants. They had come with high hopes and expectations of a life far better than the one they had left. But they were physically ill-prepared for pioneer life. They had trouble adapting to the heat and humidity of south central Texas. The diet of cornbread and meat, with almost no vegetables, was unfamiliar and diseases such as cholera and scurvy became commonplace.

The immigrants were extremely angry at the Noblemen's Society and blamed it for the conditions they lived with. Instead of 160 to 320 acres, the settlers received 10 acres. The necessities of life, promised at minimum cost, were too expensive for most people. Instead of promised protection from nearby Indians, the immigrants were always subject to attacks and had to organize their own defense.

The pressures from fear, fatigue, illness, and anger led many of the settlers to heavy drinking. For them it was the one way to overcome the troubles they found in their new life. Those who did not leave their religion behind in Germany soon forgot it once they reached Texas. Nowhere among the first immigrants were there pastors to nurture the spiritual life of the people. There were occasional American ministers who traveled through the frontier communities preaching, but their message sounded more like American nationalism than the hope that comes from the gospel of Jesus Christ.[2]

## A Call for Help Is Heard

By 1850 there were perhaps 10,000 Germans in Texas, many of them Protestants. Yet there is no record of a single Lutheran pastor in Texas until 1850. A "free Protestant" pastor named L. C. Ervendberg had accepted the invitation of Prince Carl of Solms to provide services for the immigrants at Indianola in 1844. He later accompanied them to New Braunfels. Others of a similar theological orientation ministered to some of the immigrants in Fredericksburg, Frelsburg, Galveston, Cat Spring, and elsewhere.

In 1850 the Lutheran Synod of South Carolina sent Pastor G. F. Guebner to analyze the missionary needs and opportunities in Texas. He stopped in Galveston, where he organized a congregation. Also in 1850, Pastor Caspar Braun arrived in Houston from Pennsylvania. He organized a congregation there which he served for the next 30 years. Braun became, in 1851, one of the founders and first president of the First Evangelical Lutheran Synod in Texas.

In 1849 a German colonist in Texas wrote to his relatives complaining of the lack of Christian education and opportunity to worship. Another colonist who had settled in Fredericksburg and married a Comanche Indian woman wrote to his kinfolk in Germany about the Indians' need for education. Many such letters concerning the physical and spiritual distress in Texas began to circulate in Germany. By God's grace, some of them came to

Christian F Spittler
1782-1867

the attention of Christian Friedrich Spittler, leader of a group of German Christians near Basel, Switzerland. It was through his response that the original Lutheran church organization in Texas came to be.

Spittler was born in Wimsheim (near Stuttgart), Germany, in 1782, the son of a pastor. In 1801 he joined a group called the Association of German Christians, located in Basel. There he found his life's calling. The group was founded in 1780 for the purpose of keeping the church free from the influence of ratio nalism. The rationalists were claiming that people should live their lives according to what was reasonable to the human mind, not according to belief in a supernatural being.

The Association of German Christians consisted of clergy and laity who saw it as their mission to insure that people continued to hear the Word of God in its truth and purity. Members of the Association traveled throughout German-speaking Europe giving lectures, organizing Bible studies, and leading discussion groups. A journal was started and sent throughout Europe. An intense program of correspondence was organized, with the Association functioning as the distribution center for letters to be exchanged throughout Germany.

### Spittler and Ministry

By 1808 Spittler's charisma and special ability to communicate earned him the position of secretary of the Association; he was now responsible for the group's operation. He saw the Association's task as the revitalizing of faith within Christian people. He understood the need to minister to the whole person: when people were suffering physically their material needs had to be met as well as their spiritual needs.

Spittler said that the most significant moment in his life was when he realized that by the grace of God through Jesus Christ he was a forgiven sinner. Assured of his salvation, he decided there was no work too hard, no moment too discouraging, no distance too great to keep him from fulfilling his mission. He wrote, ''It is my greatest desire and foremost intention to serve the Lord and allow myself to be used by him as he wills; wherever he calls me, there I will go.''[3]

In 1816, Spittler's Association opened a school which would train men for missionary service. His intention was not to separate men from their regular jobs. Instead he called for volunteers who would be willing to study Scripture for up to six months and then return to their normal employment. He wanted laborers, carpenters, bricklayers, any sort of craftsmen who would be willing to study the Bible and return to their jobs with a vital faith and a personal witness to co-workers.

The skills Spittler wanted his trainees to have were a clear knowledge of the Scriptures and the ability to discuss the Word with others so that they would come to understand and believe. They must also be able to work hard at a trade so that they could make a living. He said, "Be faithful in your daily work and while working attempt to enter into those places which are the shadows of Christendom, and do what you can to bring the light of Jesus Christ into those places to awaken the people to a new faith in Jesus Christ.[4]

Spittler's school became well known and his trainees were in demand throughout Germany. Later he sent missionaries to other nations of Europe—France, Belgium, and Austria—and by the 1840s they were also going to Africa, the Middle East, and Armenia. Because of his insistence on meeting the present needs of people, Spittler also organized other public service institutions: an infirmary for those seriously wounded in wars, a school for educating teachers, a school for the deaf, an orphanage, a children's hospital, several libraries, and a home for deacons. Most of these institutions are still in operation today.

### Pilgrims' Mission of St. Chrischona

In 1839 Spittler received permission from the canton of Basel to move his mission school to the chapel called St. Chrischona, atop a hill in a small village called Bettingen. A legend about the chapel reports that 11,000 virgins went on a pilgrimage to Rome in the 11th century. Many of them died as they were returning. One of those who died was named Chrischona. She was placed

St. Chrischona in 1840

on a cart pulled by oxen and the instructions were to bury her wherever the ox cart stopped. When the oxen stopped at the top of a hill, Chrischona was buried there and a chapel was built in her memory. This hill became a place of pilgrimage for those who were ill and seeking healing. It is known that the chapel existed in the 14th century because it is referred to in writings of that time.

In 1504 the virgin Chrischona was made a saint. But because the Protestant Reformation shortly after had an impact on that region of Germany and Switzerland, the chapel of St. Chrischona was no longer a place of pilgrimage and was forgotten. Farmers in the area used the chapel to store their wheat. During the Thirty Years' War the windows were torn out and the lead used for ammunition. It was not until Spittler moved in with his first missionary student in 1840 that the old chapel on the hill was renovated. Here Spittler began the missionary school which still exists today: Pilgrims' Mission—St. Chrischona.

Initially, Spittler saw the purpose of the mission school to be the same as before it moved to St. Chrischona. He wanted to train craftsmen so they would have a solid biblical foundation and a sense of Christian piety; they would then return to the work force in their own communities, among friends and relatives, their lives a witness to Jesus Christ. But within a short time the demand for his students grew. They were asked to distribute biblical literature in schools and hospitals, to teach children, to lead adult Bible study courses. Spittler realized he would have to change the level of education at St. Chrischona. He restructured the program to prepare students to be teachers of religion, catechists, deacons, and pastors' helpers.

Spittler received calls for graduates from many lands, including the United States. Between 1846 and 1849 he sent 11 graduates to North America. Caspar Braun, who had attended the mission school for only five weeks, was one of them. He went to the Pittsburgh Synod in 1847, where he was licensed to conduct services for a parish in Beaver and New Castle, Pennsylvania. In 1850 he would move to Texas, where he would soon become the first president of the Lutheran Synod in Texas.

By the late 1840s, Spittler was hearing that the greatest need was for pastors, especially among German immigrants in the United States. And that is the program to which St. Chrischona turned. As a theological seminary, St. Chrischona was unusual, for it did not affiliate with any particular denomination. Staff, faculty, and students came from both Lutheran and Reformed sources in Europe. St. Chrischona would claim only that it was Protestant and that its emphasis was upon the story of salvation presented in the Gospels. Even today this is true of the Pilgrims' Mission—St. Chrischona. It claims only to want to assist the mainline churches in reaching out to meet the spiritual needs of the people.

Thus, St. Chrischona in the middle of the 19th century gave its students the freedom to choose which church they would serve upon graduation. Many of them in the 1850s and beyond chose to work with Lutherans in the state of Texas. Spittler never sought to develop a Lutheran Synod in Texas and no official or legal ties ever existed, but the emotional bonds were strong for at least 50 years. Those first pastors who founded the Synod in Texas would often recall their student days at St. Chrischona, the fellowship they had enjoyed there, the support and guidance received from their teachers, and especially the example of faith and commitment to ministry set for them by Christian Friedrich Spittler.

### *1850: Braun, Kleis, and Sager*

When Spittler learned of the dire needs among Germans in Texas for pastoral care, he decided that St. Chrischona should respond by making Texas its priority. Before he sent anyone directly to Texas, however, two other Lutheran pastors had already arrived. One was Caspar Braun, a St. Chrischona product who was ordained by the Pittsburgh Synod in 1850 and sent to serve in Texas. The other was G. F. Guebner, whom the Lutheran Synod of South Carolina had sent to Texas in 1850 to survey missionary needs and opportunities. He arrived in Galveston and organized a congregation among the Germans there. Guebner also wrote to Spittler, asking him to send a dozen pastors to work in Texas. Guebner did not remain in Texas, however, and was not a part of the group that organized the Lutheran Synod in 1851.

The first two young men chosen by Spittler to go to Texas were Theobald G. Kleis and Christoph Adam Sager. Both were born in 1826, Kleis in Baden and Sager in Württemberg. Normally, certified graduates of St. Chrischona would go to their place of service and be ordained by the church body there. But in Texas there was no church body and no one of proper authority to perform the ordination.

Thus it was that on March 17, 1850, both Kleis and Sager were ordained by an evangelical pastor named Rink at Loerrach, Baden. They then spent several months gaining practical experience in church educational work before sailing for Texas. Shortly before they left, a gathering in Basel bade them farewell from St. Chrischona. Among the documents presented was one which is extant among Sager's descendants; a part of it reads:

> Those whose names are affixed below verify that Christoph Adam Sager, who has been a student at the Pilgrims' Mission at St. Chrischona near Basel for approximately two years and who has pursued the study course of that institution sufficiently, has, after passing his examination, been ordained to the Gospel ministry upon authorization of the Grand-duchy of Baden. . . . They also verify that in life and conduct he has demonstrated a truly Christian character, that in various branches of personal and social mission work he has demonstrated all due loyalty. He is now following a call to the state of Texas . . . that there, in cooperation with a faithful associate from the same institution he might begin an evangelical mission and work particularly among the Indians.[5]

The paper is signed by three St. Chrischona teachers and by Christian Friedrich Spittler "as the oldest member of the Mission," and is dated August 20, 1850.

In about two months, Kleis and Sager arrived at Galveston. Pastor Guebner, who had written to ask Spittler for help, had already left Texas. The two newcomers decided to move inland, to Victoria, where they worked together for a few months. Then they decided to separate. Sager would remain in the Victoria area and Kleis would go north to New Braunfels. Sager soon began serving a group of Lutherans at Meyersville, northwest of Victoria, where he remained for four years. Kleis became pastor in the settlements of Neighborsville and Hortontown, a few miles northeast of New Braunfels; he served there until 1852 when he moved to Pennsylvania for health reasons. He founded Zion Lutheran Church in Johnstown, but died in 1853 at the age of 27.

## *1851: A Whole Class to Texas*

Sometime in late 1850 Sager and Kleis sent a first report to St. Chrischona. It prompted Spittler to include this note in his missionary publication early in 1851:

> You will recall that last year we sent two of our students to Texas. Within a short time they gathered small groups about themselves and have found much work. Yes, they have seen a vision of so large a field of service that they consider it a necessity to ask that six brethren be sent to join them. . . . We are convinced that the Lord has assigned our Chrischona a field of service in that land. Looking up to Him we have decided that this year's entire class, consisting of six members, shall go there.[6]

The six were John George Ebinger, 23; Christian Oefinger, 26; John Conrad Roehm, 29; William T. Strobel, 27; Henry Wendt, 26; and Philipp Frederick Zizelmann, 26. Wendt was from Westphalia, the other five from Württemberg, the German region to the north of Switzerland. The six would be ordained by Pastor Rink before leaving Germany, on June 29, 1851. They then spent approximately two months in parish internship experiences. On September 2 they sailed from Bremen, arriving in Galveston on November 5. They were received by seven Lutheran families, members of the small congregation Pastor Guebner had started. Within a day they made the decision that Wendt would remain in Galveston with the small shepherdless flock, and the other five would go to Houston to consult with Pastor Caspar Braun about areas of service for them.

They reached Houston on November 8 and located Braun, who introduced them to Johann Braschler, a candidate for ordination who had been born in Switzerland. He had studied at the University of Bern, then came to the United States in 1848. The seven of them agreed that day, a Saturday, that on the following

Monday they would meet to discuss the possibility of organizing a Lutheran synod.

On Monday morning, November 10, the seven men met at the Presbyterian Church in Houston. Wendt in Galveston had been notified and he was able to arrive by Tuesday. Kleis and Sager were too far away to be able to join the group, though they became part of the synod shortly thereafter.

### November 10: The Synod Is Born

When the seven gathered they decided unanimously that they would organize a Lutheran church and that it would be called "First Evangelical Lutheran Synod in Texas." They elected as officers Braun (president), Zizelmann (secretary), and Roehm (treasurer). The next step was to draw a constitution. Since Braun had been a member of the Pittsburgh Synod it was suggested they use its constitution as a model. With a few minor changes, it became the Texas Synod's constitution.

The men met for three days, closing their session on Wednesday the 12th. It all happened with remarkable speed. It is worth noting some of the extraordinary features of what was done. A Lutheran synod had been formed by seven pastors and one candidate for ordination (no lay persons were involved). They were between the ages of 23 and 32. Six of them had arrived from Germany less than a week earlier, after two months at sea. Only two of the eight even had congregations to serve.

For the initial 10 leaders (including Kleis and Sager), the formation of the synod made them a team, a community. It was a visual reminder that they were not alone but were the church, an organized expression of the body of Christ called into mission. But they did not yet all have assignments. Braun remained with his congregation in Houston, and Wendt returned to the group in Galveston. Kleis and Sager were at work in the New Braunfels and Meyersville communities, respectively. What of the others?

Braschler worked in a secular trade for a time, then succeeded Kleis at Neighborsville-Hortontown near New Braunfels and was ordained in 1854.

Ebinger went to Spring Creek, a congregation near the present town of Tomball, some 25 miles northwest of Houston.

Oefinger began his ministry at Castroville and Quihi on the Medina River west of San Antonio.

Roehm landed in La Grange, a community about halfway between Houston and New Braunfels.

Strobel became pastor of a congregation in Victoria.

Zizelmann went to San Antonio, where the work was especially difficult. It was six years before he was able to organize St. John Lutheran Church; it continues to this day as the mother congregation of The American Lutheran Church in San Antonio.

These pioneer pastors suffered many hardships. The south Texas climate was not congenial to several of these northern Europeans. Five of them (Kleis, Braschler, Wendt, Zizelmann, Strobel) moved to states in the North and served congregations there. Ebinger, for health reasons, returned to Europe and continued his ministry there. These six were gone from Texas within the first decade.[7]

All of them, and those who followed, lived with poor housing and extremely low pay. They had to walk and ride horseback over long distances. They were often ill, with few doctors available. And they suffered from loneliness. Ebinger wrote to St. Chrischona in 1855:

> It has been almost a year since I wrote last and still I have received no reply to any of my letters. We live in a land in which true and honest friends are few; sometimes it seems as though there are none. For that reason we think of our old friends all the more. But when we do not hear from them for years, we do at times feel as though we have only one friend in all the world—the best one of all—Him in heaven. Even though I have very little income, I would

gladly pay $3 annually for postage to get letters from my dear teachers and superiors.[8]

St. Chrischona did not abandon the Texans, despite Ebinger's empty mailbox. Spittler would die in 1867, but his institution continued to send pastors for the rest of the 19th century. Between 70 and 80 more were to come to Texas from the Pilgrims' Mission before the relationship ended in the 1890s.

## Affiliation with Iowa

From the start, the Synod in Texas felt overwhelmed by the large missionary challenge it faced. Combining that with a sense of isolation from other Lutherans, concentrated in the North and East, the Texas Lutherans sought broader affiliations. Already in 1853 they joined the General Synod, a federation of eastern Lutheran groups, hoping to receive badly needed pastors from that affiliation. "When the Synod in Texas broke from the General Synod in 1868, failure to receive that help was as important a factor as the anticonfessional movement within the General Synod."[9]

By the 1880s, the Synod in Texas was seriously looking for Lutherans in the Midwest with which it might form a relationship. In 1889, it authorized its president to contact the Missouri, Iowa, and Ohio Synods to explore affiliation possibilities. For several years the debate in the Texas group was conducted, with four options: remain independent or affiliate with one of the three Midwest German-origin synods.

In 1895 it was decided to ask to be accepted as a district of the Iowa Synod. Iowa agreed at its 1896 convention and the Synod in Texas confirmed the agreement when it met later that same year. The Texas affiliation with Iowa was not a complete absorption into the larger body. The Synod in Texas continued to be known as the "district-synod" of Texas and maintained a large amount of autonomy in its internal affairs. It relied on the Iowa

Synod's leadership, however, in all matters pertaining to external affairs. Thus, the Texas district-synod was not a direct party to the negotiations leading to the 1930 formation of the American Lutheran Church.

One of the reasons Texas sought a formal affiliation with another Lutheran body was its need for theological education for its pastors. The Synod in Texas was never able to develop its own theological seminary. For much of the first half century, it relied on a supply of pastors from Europe. Its own native-grown pastors were sent to various Lutheran seminaries in the United States. A number of them were trained at Iowa's Wartburg Seminary in Dubuque. After the 1896 affiliation, Wartburg formally became the theological school for the Texas district-synod.

Between 1851 and 1896, the Synod in Texas grew to 40 congregations with 40 pastors. When the ALC was formed in 1930, the Texas district-synod numbered 161 congregations, 102 pastors, and nearly 38,000 baptized members (7% of the new church's membership).

The Synod in Texas is a distinctive story in U.S. Lutheranism, just as Texas the state has a distinctive history. Unlike most of the other stories in this collection, that of the Synod in Texas has almost no conflict with other varieties of Lutherans. Its struggles rather centered around planting the church in an alien culture, adjusting to an unfamiliar climate, and maintaining a Lutheran identity in a sea of indifference. And many of the nominal Lutherans from Germany were part of that apathetic tide.

That the Synod in Texas was born, grew strong, and continues to witness through its descendants is itself testimony to God's gracious ways in planting and extending the church.

# 5

Norwegian (1853)

# The Gentry Tradition—Men and Women of a Leadership Class

## How Shall the Faith and Human Culture Interrelate?

by Leigh D. Jordahl

### *October 1853*

Germans in Texas are nearing the close of their second year together in the Evangelical Lutheran Synod of Texas. Another small band of Germans (2 pastors, 18 lay persons) will arrive this month in Dubuque, Iowa, from Michigan to form, less than a year hence, the Evangelical Lutheran Synod of Iowa.

In southern Wisconsin a gathering of pastors and lay delegates representing 17 Norwegian congregations is occurring at Luther Valley (near today's Beloit in Rock County). On October 3 through 7, they organize the Norwegian Evangelical Lutheran Church of America. The second such organization among Norwegian-Lutheran immigrants, it soon becomes the largest and most stable.

### *Gentlemen on the Frontier*

The story of Norwegian-American Lutheranism has been told more than once as a story that, to contemporary Lutherans, must appear to be one of schismatic contentiousness. We live in an age that can engage lustily in political polemics but generally has a strong aversion to theological polemics. These Norwegians, all from one state church in the home country, all settling about the same time in the same northern Midwest communities, found it impossible throughout the 19th century to get together in one church on this continent. That despite the fact that all earnestly believed in unity.

The stormy history has been documented most carefully by E. Clifford Nelson and Eugene Fevold.[1] At the very center of most of the controversies stood the Norwegian Synod and its theological warhorses—all of whom arrived in the decade between 1848 and 1857 and headed for the Norwegian settlements in southern Wisconsin and northeastern Iowa. They included H. A. Stub (arrived 1848), H. A. Preus (1851), J. A. O. Ottesen (1852), U. V. Koren (1853), and Laur. Larsen (1857). This look at the early years of the Norwegian Synod will focus on men like these—and the women who accompanied them—as they struggled to keep faith and culture together in frontier farm communities.

The Norwegian Synod has not always enjoyed a good press. It has often been portrayed, even if unintentionally, as a kind of aristocratic and doctrinaire mischief maker. Its alliance with the Missouri Synod was never popular, even within its own constituency. Its fervent emphasis on pure doctrine has been characterized as commitment to scholastic orthodoxy (and, by implication, "dead orthodoxy"), while its emphasis on traditional liturgical forms, its stress on churchly decency and order, and its careful regulation of lay activity were frequently seen as representing formalism and clericalism.

The Synod's spirit did not appear to fit the antiformalistic, egalitarian impulses so popularly, even if romantically, characterized as the frontier mentality. And the fact that Synod leaders in their own minds opposed formalism, clericalism, and certainly anything like dead orthodoxy does not change the unfortunate fact of how they were perceived.

H. A. Preus
1825-1894

The Norwegian Synod did tend in almost all the controversies that embroiled it for a half century or more to take stands that were sure to put it at odds with its own environment. There was emerging among the Norwegian immigrants an egalitarianism, with its suspicion of the learned gentry class; a growing affinity for the patterns and thought forms and anti-abstractionism of the American democratic faith; a certain attachment, already inherited from Norwegian pietism and dramatically reinforced by the ethos of the frontier, to practical, experiential religiosity; a hostility to anything that appeared hierarchical (in fact, a kind of anti-clericalism); and, most emphatically, dislike for theological forms that implied determinism or minimized human freedom to shape one's destiny.

### Using Sunday and Using Wine

American frontier experience was a loud assertion of human ingenuity and opportunity for social and economic mobility. "Class," for all its reality, has always been a dirty word in the

United States. Furthermore, Synod theology, like that of the New England Puritans earlier, was static, carefully structured without loose ends, and given to keen intellectual reflection. It required expertise and was best practiced by the gentleman with sufficient training to exercise the life of the mind.

In instance after instance these gentlemen leaders of the Synod came down on the side of things least compatible with their environment. Nor did the Synod manage, as did Missouri under the remarkable leadership of C. F. W. Walther, to make a virtue of the vice of being so different, thereby ingeniously building a strong esprit de corps.

Already in 1859 debate erupted over lay preaching, and already then the most the Synod leaders would concede to such activity was lay preaching in emergency situations (like lay Baptism), and even then only if the preacher had some theological expertise. There was discussion about the "Christian Sunday" and again, though not promoting Sunday work, the Synod came down unambiguously against what it saw as pietistic legalism. Thus, for instance, the daughters of Laur. Larsen were envied by their non-Synod friends in Decorah, Iowa, because the Larsen girls could play paper dolls or do handwork on Sundays.

So also the Synod had little sympathy for the more rigorous temperance impulses. A story is reliably told of Ingerid Markkus, wife of an early Synod pastor at Norway Lake, Minnesota. She was a strong-minded woman known for her serious view of the moral life. No friend of the saloon, she was sometimes invited to parish homes where a well-meaning host or hostess offered her a glass of wine. She winced inwardly, drank it politely, and defended herself by saying, "Wine in itself is no sin, but it is a sin to hurt the feelings of someone who means to be showing you honor."

That same woman, after the untimely death of her husband, went to the University of Minnesota, then taught English and history at the Synod's Lutheran Ladies Seminary at Red Wing, and was a regular contributor to Norwegian-American newspapers. She saw it as a goal to train ladies who could marry gentlemen pastors. Red Wing Seminary itself was perceived as a kind of genteel finishing school.

## Slavery No Sin?

Far more disastrous for the Synod was its unfortunate involvement in the slavery question. The Synod leaders had no loyalty to the South (though Laur. Larsen, president of Luther College, was a states' rights defender) and certainly had no affection for slavery. Moreover, Abraham Lincoln was later held in almost idolistic affection and, according to good sources, few Synod school buildings did not have him prominently pictured.

Nevertheless, when faced with the pointed question, Laur. Larsen spoke for the Synod in declaring that ''slavery is not in itself a sin.'' The position taken was actually only an extension of the position on Sunday and temperance. It was akin to the position adopted by the Missouri Synod and was based on the fact that the Bible does not condemn the institution of slavery. It was precisely identical with that of a contemporary group or person which, when faced with the abortion phenomenon, declares abortion to be a moral evil but, lacking a clear biblical prohibition, refuses to label it as always or in every circumstance a sin. Yet the Synod's stand was heard as a defense of an ugly institution, and it caused major consternation among its own laity and in certain other Lutheran bodies.[2]

An even more major controversy followed when, in the 1880s, the strife over predestination surfaced. In keeping with its Augustinian tradition, the Synod adopted a position, meant to affirm the objectivity of grace, that emphatically negated human free will as having any role in salvation. The position appeared to deny human responsibility. Moreover, the Synod position was perceived as a Lutheranized version of Calvinistic double predestination.

There were other issues as well, and the Synod fought a hard battle on all of them. It failed dismally, for instance, in its attempts to found a parochial school system similar to that of the Missouri Synod (where it worked so successfully). The fact remains, however, that for all its seriousness about theological exactness and its zeal to proclaim a gospel of comfort, the Synod did not manage to sponsor the kind of broad churchmanship mixing American democratic idealism and workable Lutheran self-identity that the times required. The story of success on that score belongs with the Synod opponents who in the 1890s formed the United Norwegian Lutheran Church and rallied around St. Olaf College (see Chapter 8). By 1917 the Norwegian Synod, originally the major group among Norwegian Americans, was a minority movement.[3]

### The Gentry Tradition

However, too much attention has probably been paid to the Synod's theological tradition. Not enough has been given—except to see it in the bad sense as "aristocratic tendencies"—to the Synod as representing what can be called "the gentry tradition of noble service." Like the Puritan leaders (who got into troubles not unlike those of the Synod and, as with Synod leaders, were suspected of class snobbery), the Synod founders represented the old tradition of Christian humanism. They assumed also that no such tradition can survive without a strong leadership class. Nor, unlike American populism, did such people discount the expert, the intellectual, or the gentlemen and ladies who help pass on a tradition. Not for one moment did such people imagine religion as an enemy of the mind. Neither should it be so that religion stands against the good, the true, the beautiful in human culture.

Noblesse oblige—the obligation to be noble—is laid precisely on those who have been privileged with education. As university-educated men, the Synod leaders in founding Luther College (1861) followed closely the European classical humanist model.

Nor is it surprising that they took as their model the European humanistic, classical tradition. Thus Latin and Greek were stressed. In doing this the Luther College curriculum was similar to that of the Missouri Synod colleges, where the classics were also emphasized. Yet in so doing the Missourians were thinking of the curriculum in distinctly preprofessional terms. At Luther College the classical curriculum was used not so much to provide technical preparation for reading theology (though, to be sure, it did that too) as to employ it as an avenue for penetrating and appreciating the best that human beings had said and thought. In so doing the Synod decided for the liberal arts. In so doing the Synod was also attacked for its "humanistic" tendencies.[4]

Although the intention was above all to produce ministers, the Synod self-consciously (again in distinction from the Missourians, as well as from the very different but also preprofessional program at Augsburg College) decided that a college must be an entity in itself. Therefore, attempts to locate a seminary in Decorah were resisted.[5] From the very beginning at Luther College, fees and curriculum were identical for students whether or not they were preparing for seminary. In short, as at Harvard College earlier, the Synod took what it regarded as the best model for producing a leadership class.

As representatives from what had become in Norway the *conditionert* or educated class, made up of military officers, judicial people, and clergy, the Synod leaders stood distinct from the rich farmer class that owned property (few of whom came to America) and the *husmand* or poorest class that served the upper class and the wealthy farmers. The nonclergy American immigrants came mostly from the lowest class. Obviously then there was a major class distinction between Synod leadership and its constituency. Yet, it should also be noted that the men and women from the educated class who chose to come to the United States represented exactly the best of the ideals affirmed by their class. That is, only a strong idealism and a very firmly grounded commitment to service could attract such people to the primitive frontier, far from home, culture, and social intercourse with their own kind. In Norway the upper classes frowned on emigration; thus no romantic prestige went along with the decision to leave Norway. So, in a sense, these Synod leaders represented the cream of their class.

## Women as Transplanters

As remarkable as anything, and practically ignored in official histories, was the crucial role of women in this venture of transplanting faith and culture. The early Synod *prestefruen* (pastors' wives), themselves members of the *conditionert* class, were mostly women of refinement, keen intelligence and, in a sense, executive managers of things. In no sense could they be considered useless ornaments (as a Nora saw herself in Ibsen's *Doll House*) or captives to the kind of middle-class "feminine mystique" so vividly described by a Betty Friedan a century later.

Diderikke Ottesen Brandt may not have been entirely typical but neither was her background unique. The daughter of a pastor who was also a college dean, she spent three years at the Moravian Ladies School in Schleswig, Denmark, and also traveled widely in Europe. She appears to have been a much stronger personality than her husband, Pastor Nils Brandt. She lived on the Luther College campus for almost 20 years until events caused her husband's early retirement. During most of those years she functioned in fact as the first lady of the college (the wife of President Larsen was for years in poor health and, aside from that, was of a retiring nature).

What Mrs. Brandt did was to furnish the young men a kind of home away from home where, for instance, at her regular Sunday afternoon social events the boys were invited as guests. More important, Mrs. Brandt self-consciously took upon herself the

Diderikke Brandt
1827-1885

task of teaching her young friends appreciation for music and conversation, the proprieties and niceties of gracious living without, however, even the slightest trace of snobbery or artificiality. Clearly, Mrs. Brandt saw herself as an important adjunct to the educational aims of the school. And it is quite clear that the male leadership of the college was happy to have her do her job (though there are hints that some of the Synod pastors' wives saw her as somewhat pushy). Years later a major building on the Luther campus was named after her.

If one is to say something about the role of women in the Synod's attempt to establish a Christian culture among the Norwegian immigrants, one must be careful to state that documentary evidence is not abundant. Furthermore, neither Synod pastors nor their wives were in any sense ideological critics of inherited patterns of male and female roles. Certainly anything like today's feminist movement would have baffled them. Never did they even conceive of women pastors, although—again in very sharp contrast to the German Lutherans in the Midwest—they found no difficulty at all in encouraging women to assume positions of importance at the educational institutions they founded. This stance was supported solidly even by the most rigorously orthodox of the Synod men.

As an interesting illustration, a small group of Synod people refused to enter the Norwegian merger of 1917 because, they maintained, doctrine had been compromised. They then organized what was commonly called the "Little Synod," with headquarters at Bethany College in Mankato, Minnesota. Its president was Sigurd Ylvisaker, a gentleman scholar and also an orthodontist of the first rank. For having women as full faculty members in the central disciplines, he was criticized by his Wisconsin and Missouri Synod associates; at their schools women could teach only on the elementary level. Ylvisaker stood his ground by appealing to his Synod tradition and its view of college as *in loco parentis*. In commenting on the criticism, this writer recalls that he used to say, "Why, we always knew how important the women were. Maybe that's why they [the German pastors] are so uncouth. They've been shortchanged in their educations."

### Gender Roles

The public and private worlds known to the 19th century Synod leadership class were radically different from those of the 20th century: quite obviously so in almost all respects, but obviously so also in relation to gender roles. Certainly, no Synod leader or his wife doubted for a moment that the man was the head of the family and its public spokesman. Nor would any of them have been anything but offended if someone had suggested removing the "obey" promise from the wedding liturgy. (They did, however, ingeniously demythologize the word by insisting that in a good marriage two people are so happily bound that they will the same thing and thus "obedience" is never an issue.)

Yet gender roles were very different among Synod leadership people, compared to what would later be considered normal. In the world of 20th-century life, at least before the feminist movement of the past few decades, a sharp distinction existed between what Monika Hellwig calls the "intimate and immediate level" and the "public level." [6] We might note also how there has been a very steady movement away from *Gemeinschaft* (community of shared values) to *Gesellschaft* (association of increasing impersonality and bureaucratization). The public and the private have been purposely separated, with women typically consigned to the private. There, at the intimate level, women experience great freedom to express feeling, emotion, warmth, graciousness, and importance.

At the public level, however, feminine virtues can be turned exactly into vices. At that level a person is important on entirely different terms. Primary importance is attached to disinterested rationality and to economic, social, political, and power structures. Alienation and consequently justified perceptions of oppression occur when the intimate is declared peripheral by the more importantly perceived public level. The woman may be seen hardly at all as a person of genuine significance in that world which really counts. Most significant is the fact that it is at the public level that real value is recognized and rewarded. The married woman may be seen only as an adjunct to someone else. Males perform the important roles. Of course, one may be satisfied to live in intimate spheres, but that becomes increasingly difficult and most difficult precisely for those who are part of a leadership class and have been taught to value the life of the mind.

The temptation, applying this to the Synod leadership class of the 19th century, would be to overrate the case and make Synod pastors' wives some kind of precursors of modern liberated women. They obviously were not that. It would be equally unfair to suggest that only the Synod, among the Norwegian-Lutheran groups, allowed ministers' wives a role of high importance.

Yet, given the distinctly gentry tradition of the first and second generation Synod leadership, the dichotomy between public and private was held in balance. The ministerial society represented by such well-known names as Preus, Larsen, Otteson, Brandt, Stub, Hjort, Torgerson, Reque, Ylvisaker, Naesseth, and numerous others was a society in which public and private were closely intertwined. Pastors, of course, were the official representatives. They did the public speaking and voting; in no sense were the wives "assistant pastors" (the rather demeaning role sometimes later placed on such wives).

### The Frontier Parsonage

The women had their own role and it required high skill. The center of day by day life, also the place where the ministers studied and carried on their theological conversation with other ministers, was the parsonage. The women ran the home and it was precisely there in the home that the crucial civilizing work went on. The parsonage was the symbolic center of life and in it husband and wife were partners with, if one is to take seriously the accounts we have, women mostly in charge. It is interesting, for instance, to discover how extraordinarily practical some of those gently educated women became about technical matters of farm management and economic calculating. Nor, as the sketches of Linka Preus illustrate, did they disappear into the background when their husbands carried on their discussions.[7]

Those were the days of mostly life-long settled pastorates and before the days of numerous committees, interest groups, and specialization of functions. The high prestige parishes were rural and almost no pastor served just one congregation. Neither did any pastor have a study except in the parsonage. In any event, the parsonage was the unifying center of both the intimate and

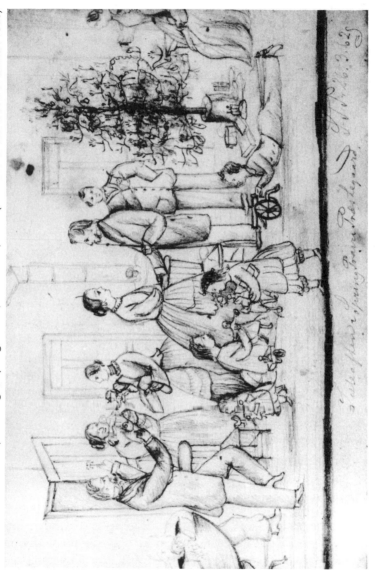

Christmas at the Preus parsonage, Spring Prairie, Wisconsin, 1862 (from the Sketchbook of Linka Preus)

the public life. In some instances, especially for the daughters who had as yet no good schools to attend beyond the local public school, it also served as a center for education.

The husbands were often gone for long periods of time. The women kept things going and, however hard they worked, they must have known full well how important they were. In fact, they did enjoy high prestige in their own right. Culture and practical know-how were passed on through the parsonage. One might say that the parsonage served something like the monastery in medieval days—the place where the best of the tradition was preserved and cultivated and thus a kind of sign that there is more to life than only meat and drink. More than just piety too!

The burdens on the wives were tremendous, requiring as they did not only the genteel graces of restraint, balance, moderation, and love of beauty but also skill of management and enormous inner resources of character. To a remarkable degree such women as Linka Preus, Elizabeth Koren, Christiane Hjort (*prestefrue* at the Paint Creek parish and known throughout the Synod for the gracious parsonage she maintained), Diderikke Brandt, and Dena Torgerson (sister of the famous Rasmus Anderson and, by good accounts, not far behind him in holding strong opinions) all maintained a vision of faith and the good life joined together. They tried to pass the vision on to the parishioners. Depending as they did upon hired help (who were not, however, considered maids or servants as they had been in Norway), they often chose bright, promising young girls of confirmation age and brought them into their families.

### Parsonage as Escape

An interesting story was told by a minister's widow, then in her eighties, about how she "escaped" (as she pointedly put it) from what she feared was her destiny. T. A. Torgerson, pastor at Lake Mills, Iowa, sized her up as a young girl of promise. So she was invited into the Torgerson home and was pushed hard to do something with her keen mind. Off she went to Luther Academy in Albert Lea, Minnesota, then to the Lutheran Normal School at Sioux Falls, South Dakota. She had a happy career as a teacher until she herself married a Synod pastor. Never did she quit praising the Torgersons.

A hard life it must have been. Also a discouraging life for idealistic immigrants from a gentry tradition that was destined, both theologically and culturally, to have a hard time on American soil. Already by the second generation, most certainly by the third, the Synod represented a kind of rearguard action. Widely known as conservatives (they also regarded themselves thus, with pride) the Synod leaders were sometimes perceived as reactionaries.

At the time of the predestination controversy, several ministerial families were ousted from their parsonages as pastors were deposed from office. Pushed by the urgent need for pastors, the Synod was forced to compromise its stringent educational ideals. A "practical course" was introduced as an alternative preparation for the ministry for those who lacked the desired humanistic liberal arts education.

Aside from Luther College, which remained a school for men only until 1936, the Synod schools established either for women (Lutheran Ladies Seminary at Red Wing, Minnesota) or for both men and women (all the academies, the Sioux Falls Normal School, and Park Region College in Fergus Falls, Minnesota) failed to achieve academic distinction. Rather, Synod families desiring a top education for their daughters had to send them off to non-Lutheran universities (as, for instance, the granddaughters of U. V. and Elizabeth Koren). In some instances the children, male and female, who went to secular schools of quality were not able later to feel at home in the religious atmosphere of the Synod.

### *Faith Plus Culture Equals Noble Service*

Yet as long as the dream seemed a reality—a dream of order, culture, orthodox faith, and vital piety joined together—the Synod was an interesting experiment of merging faith and culture in such a way as to produce noble service.

By the 1890s the first generation of Synod leaders was passing from the scene (H. A. Preus died in 1894, J. A. O. Ottesen had retired, U. V. Koren's major theological battles had been fought). The second generation must have realized that their Synod tradition was now only one among several competing for the same ethnic constituency. Yet it remained so that churchly order, liturgical appreciation, and commitment to serious dialectical theology remained primary concerns of the Synod. When the merged Norwegian Lutheran Church in America was organized in 1917 it was in no small measure indebted to the Synod for its theological vitality.

The tradition of gentility associated with the early Synod families did not perpetuate itself. Indeed, it neither could nor should have endured in the American environment. Yet Norwegian Lutherans in the United States have rarely implied that faith and culture are necessarily enemies. Nor were revivalistic tendencies toward subjectivity, although certainly present among Norwegian Lutherans, allowed to take over in such a way as to oust dialectical theological reflection and debate. It is not entirely implausible to suggest that the Synod tradition also stood as guard against tendencies to despise culture, as though the good things of this world must be seen as utterly unrelated—if not antithetical—to the world of faith.

# 6

Iowa (1854)

# M ission Martyr on the Western Frontier
## Can Cross-cultural Mission Be Achieved?

by Gerhard M. Schmutterer and Charles P. Lutz

It is July of 1860 and most residents of the United States are moving through their daily routines without much thought about Wyoming. Indeed, a majority of Americans are probably unable to give you the location of this unorganized western region, populated chiefly by bands of hunting, roaming Indians. Most of the country—North and South, back East and out West in California—is thinking about the presidential election campaign and the future of the Union. Can war between the states be prevented by any of the four candidates. Kentucky's Breckinridge, Tennessee's Bell, or one of that pair from Illinois, Douglas and Lincoln?

But in northeast Iowa there are a few people who think about Wyoming a lot. They are recent immigrants from Germany, mostly Bavarians. Less than six years earlier, they had organized a new church body, the Evangelical Lutheran Synod of Iowa and Other States. They have a dream: to bring Christianity to Indians on the western frontier. And right now that dream is being pursued by three men in the wilds of Wyoming, sent to establish a base for gospel work.

The team includes one pastor, Moritz Braeuninger, at 23 a recent graduate of the Iowa Synod's Wartburg Seminary at St. Sebald, Iowa. Trained as a carpenter in Saxony, he had been recruited by Pastor Wilhelm Loehe of Neuendettelsau to go to America, complete theological studies, and become a pastor in the young church in Iowa. Two years earlier, in 1858, Braeuninger had spent six months on an exploratory mission to the Crows in Montana and Wyoming. Others in the team are Theodore Seyler, a theological student who is referred to as Braeuninger's "mission helper," and a farmer named Beck, who is to help make the mission station self-sufficient in food.

### The Powder River Station

Since April 1860 the three have been at work on the west bank of the Powder River, opposite the drainage of the Dry Fork, in what will 30 years hence be the northeast of the new state of Wyoming. In 1860, the area is still a part of Nebraska Territory. The station is about six miles downstream (north) from a site which, in the next century, will locate a ranch-country hamlet named Sussex.

From the middle of July, Ogalala Sioux war parties have been stopping at the station, looking for Crows. The Powder River, following the Treaty of Fort Laramie (1851), is the eastern boundary of Crow territory, placing the mission station in a kind of buffer zone between the Crows and the Teton Sioux to the east. The Indians traditionally battle with each other over territorial hunting rights. But all tribes agree on one point: they are not pleased to have whites settling in the region and view it as a violation of the 1851 treaty. With solid historic precedent, they see the first isolated settlements as the beginning of a process that will end with eviction of Indians from land that is promised them forever, by treaty with the United States government. They have learned that the whites have great power, not only from guns and numbers, but power to change the mind of the government in Washington.

Braeuninger and his colleagues, however, are not on the Powder River to take Indian land. They are there to help the Indians by telling them how the God of the Christians loves them and how they can live in peace with other Indians and with white people. The missionaries have learned the basics of the Crow language and provide hospitality when groups of Indians stop by. On July 16 a small band of Ogalala comes, asks for food, and leaves. Two days later some 50 warriors, mostly Ogalala with a few Hunkpapa, appear. Their hosts prepare tea, bake bread, and make pancakes to serve them. The next day another group shows up and asks for food. Braeuninger scolds them for their outrageous begging, but eventually yields and gives them bread.

On Sunday, July 22, a war party of six comes to the station, identifying themselves as Ogalala. They spend a pleasant evening smoking and talking with the whites and stay overnight, sleeping indoors next to the missionaries. They remain through noon meal on Monday, with no sign of discontent or threat, then leave.

Braeuninger rests for a while after lunch, then suggests that Beck take a walk with him. They leave, mentioning to Seyler that they will bring back their cattle upon their return. Braeuninger takes along his rifle and says to Seyler, ''I wish you many Indians.''

### Braeuninger's Final Walk

The two walkers journey downstream, talking about their lot in the wilderness and comforting themselves with biblical thoughts, Beck later recalls. About a mile and a half north of the station they are surprised to come upon the six Indians who had left them only a few hours before, heading in the opposite direction. The Indians say they had heard a shot and suspected it was a group of enemy Blackfeet. Could they hide in the mission station? Braeuninger says the cellar would protect them and agrees to accompany them back to the station. He advises Beck to continue looking for the cattle, farther downstream.

When Beck returns to the house he learns from Seyler that neither Braeuninger nor the Indians have returned. Immediately the two men search the area, continuing into the night, but no one is found. With loaded guns, fearing they may be the next victims, they spend the night inside the house. For several more days they search the vicinity of the station. Is Braeuninger dead? Is he kidnapped? The latter, they think, is unlikely, since Indians know that holding a white captive is punishable by death.

After some days the two leave the station and travel to Deer Creek, some 100 miles south on the North Platte, the nearest center of white authority. The Indian agent there, Major Thomas Twiss, sends a man with them for protection and they return to the Powder River station for more searching. Nothing is found. No blood or sign of a struggle can be seen. No body has surfaced downstream.

Seyler and Beck return to Deer Creek to await instructions from Iowa. In September two other missionaries arrive—Carl Krebs and Georg Flachenecker—but they left Iowa unaware of the Braeuninger disappearance. Toward the end of September a man comes to Deer Creek claiming to have heard this story from a group of Ogalala at Fort Laramie:

Six members of the Hunkpapas (a branch of the Teton Sioux) stopped at the Powder River station. One of the group wished to kill the chief of the white men, if he could be found alone outside. If that were impossible, he wanted to attack the station by night and kill all three, since white settlers near the Powder River were not wanted. The rest of the group prevailed, however, and the visit was friendly, until Braeuninger and Beck met the six along the river. When Braeuninger agreed to walk back to the station with them, the six gradually fell behind. One was determined to shoot Braeuninger but the others tried to argue him out of it. As

Missionary Krebs with
Wyoming Indian boys
in Iowa, 1865

Monument at grave
of Indian boys who died
in 1865, with tribute
to martyred missionary,
Moritz Braeuninger,
at St. Sebald, Iowa

Braeuninger walked alone ahead of them, the militant one put a bullet through his back. Braeuninger's repeated attempts to get on his feet were finally stopped when the group wounded him fatally. They then mutilated his face and threw his body into the river, which was swollen and fast-flowing from heavy rains.[1]

There are other rumors: that the Indians were Ogalala, not Hunkpapa, and Braeuninger's killer was the son of a chief; that Braeuninger was killed by a bear. Whether by Ogalala or Hunkpapa, the story of the killing as heard at Fort Laramie and repeated to the missionaries at Deer Creek is the one generally accepted back in Iowa.

Today, a century and a quarter later, a mystery still hovers over the quiet valley of the Powder. Ranchers in the area are scarcely aware of the tragedy that happened there. No marker calls attention to the site of the mission station or recalls what happened a short distance downstream.

What brought this young German, a true friend of the Indian people, from Saxony to Wyoming's wilderness? What vision drove Moritz Braeuninger and those who sent him? And what happened to that vision after his death?

To answer such questions, we turn back to a small village in Bavaria, in the early 1840s.

### *Loehe and His Passion*

Wilhelm Loehe (Löhe) became pastor of a congregation in Neuendettelsau, Franconia (northern Bavaria), some 20 miles southwest of Nürnberg, in 1837. He would serve there until his death in 1872. During the 1840s and 1850s, Loehe and his co-workers saw it as their calling to provide simultaneously for the spiritual care of German immigrants in America and for the evangelization of the native American. Loehe would recruit candidates for both pastoral ministry and parish school teaching in Germany, give them preliminary training in Bavaria, then send them for completion of studies in America.

Wilhelm Loehe
1808-1872

The first men were dispatched in 1842; they affiliated with the Ohio Synod and studied theology at its seminary in Columbus. Among the next to go was a W. Hattstaedt, who arrived in 1843 and joined the small Michigan Synod. He reported to Loehe that central Michigan looked like an ideal place for Lutheran work among the Indians (Chippewa tribe) and that the Michigan Synod was already engaged in such efforts with modest help from the Lutheran Ministerium of Pennsylvania. Loehe soon sent Hattstaedt detailed instructions, including this word:

> You are requested to gain detailed information concerning the missionaries of different denominations who are laboring among the heathen Indians, and to investigate what our brethren of the household of faith have done for those tribes, and how we ourselves might cooperate with already established Indian missions. One might perhaps learn considerably from the Moravian missions, to which you will kindly direct your attention.[2]

Loehe had a magnificent vision of how to evangelize the American Indians. He would plant at the edge of the frontier entire Christian colonies, rather than single gospel-bearers, so the Indians might see everyday Christian community with their own eyes. The colonies would be centers from which the gospel's light would radiate. Hattstaedt and other early emissaries sent by Loehe suggested an area around Saginaw Bay in Michigan as a locale for the experiment. The first colony was founded in 1845 along the Cass River in Saginaw County and named Frankenmuth (Courage of the Franconians). In the years following Loehe sent several hundred colonists—farmers and tradespeople, always with pastors—and they established several more colonies in Saginaw County and to the west. Of his colonists Loehe wrote:

> Not poverty is the cause of their emigration. . . . Nothing prompts them but the thought—at once humble and sublime—of founding in the wilderness of the New World a starting point for mission work among the heathen.

The colonies became thriving centers of German Lutheranism, but as mission outposts they disappointed. As soon as the colonists settled, the Indians moved on north and west, and the colonies could not move with them. The one effort which had some success was a mission station named Bethany, opened in Gratiot County, just north of the present town of St. Louis, in 1848. (A cemetery remains today, one mile north of St. Louis on Riverside Drive.) Bethany flourished for a decade and several hundred Indians became Christians there. Bethany was closed in 1860 when the Indians were pressured into signing a treaty and moving north to a reservation in Isabella County. The mission was reorganized at Mt. Pleasant, but was abandoned in 1869.

The once promising work among Indians in Michigan was thus closed after a quarter-century, victim of denominational competition between Methodists and Lutherans, the negative example of white settlers, and the continuing removal of Indian populations. Yet, the work was not without fruit. When the community of Frankenmuth celebrated its 75th anniversary in 1920, an elderly Indian was there to offer a short address; he delivered it in German!

Other Loehe-sent teachers and pastors were serving Germans in the Fort Wayne, Indiana, area, where they founded a theological seminary in 1846. The Indiana and Michigan Loehe groups were both attracted to a colony of Saxon Lutherans who had settled in Missouri. Loehe suggested that his people unite with the Missourians—and they did. In 1847 the three groups formed what is now the Lutheran Church–Missouri Synod. Despite a disagreement between Missouri's leader, C. F. W. Walther, and Loehe six years later, the Missouri Synod today claims Loehe, justly, as a cofounder. The first suggestion of a united synod with commitment to the Lutheran confessions had come from him, as did the bulk of the original pastoral leadership: in 1849, 52 of its clergy were Loehe men, compared to only 13 from the Saxon colony.

Loehe gave the Fort Wayne seminary to the new synod and it continued to train clergy, most of whom were men sent by Loehe. But the Neuendettelsau leader wanted to supply parish teachers as well. So in 1852 he sent a Pastor Georg Grossmann and five students to open a teachers' seminary in Saginaw. The school graduated its first teacher the next year. That was also its final class—in Michigan. (The Saginaw school is considered the forerunner of both Wartburg Seminary in Dubuque, Iowa, and Wartburg College in Waverly, Iowa. On the Waverly campus, Grossmann Hall, a dormitory, recalls the Saginaw founder's name.)

### New Start in Iowa

Loehe and Walther had been carrying on a mild dispute over the doctrine of the church and the ministry. At Saginaw, Grossmann and a pastor at one of the colonies, John Deindoerfer, sided with Loehe in the conviction that one view was as "Lutheran" as the other and that the existence of differing perspectives ought not break the unity of the young Missouri Synod. The other clergy in Michigan disagreed and wrote Loehe to ask that the Saginaw teachers' school be turned over to the new synod's control or be removed to a location where Missouri had no work under way.

Apparently Iowa was the closest such spot. Just seven years into statehood, Iowa was the beginning of the West in 1853. It was there that the two pastors, with two students and 18 colonists, arrived in October 1853. They crossed the Mississippi at Dubuque and immediately reopened the school there, under Grossmann's direction. Deindoerfer and the farmers, attracted by rich land at $1.25 per acre, went 60 miles farther west to start the settlement of St. Sebald (near today's Strawberry Point). They named their community in memory of the first missionary who had carried the gospel to their ancestors in the vicinity of Nürnberg, Bavaria.

Loehe was saddened by the rupture of his work in Michigan. His letter to the Missourian clergy in the Saginaw area sounds a note that continues to mark U.S. inter-Lutheran relations into the late 20th century:

> Not my heart, only my hand is taking leave from these colonies today. I feel toward you as I always did. Even regarding the doctrine of the ministry you remain my near relatives. But far be it from me that I share your confidence as though you and your old and new authorities, through whose eyes you also read the Word of God, were right in all things. . . . We have not as yet reached any degree of finality, as you have, not because we do not know what you know, but because we are not convinced of the Scripturalness of your position.[3]

In 1854 Loehe's Iowans formed the Iowa Synod, with exactly two congregations (Dubuque and St. Sebald) and four pastors! But the young synod grew quickly. Loehe continued to send trained pastors as well as money for the school, which soon turned to preparing men for the clergy as well as parochial school teachers. Within 5 years the synod numbered 28 congregations and 25 pastors; by 1864 it counted more than 50 congregations in 7 states, with 41 clergy.

In 1857 the young seminary was moved from Dubuque to St. Sebald, location of the strongest congregation of the synod, for reasons that were primarily financial. Costs of keeping the institutional family would be lessened if a farm could furnish the school with food. When the seminary's new building was dedicated on Oct. 31, 1857, the school for the first time received a name—*Wartburg*, after the castle near Eisenach, Saxony, where Martin Luther had lived while translating the New Testament into German (1521-22). By the end of 1857 the seminary boasted 16 students. They ranged in age from 14 to the early 20s, and the full course of study included four years of preparatory work and three years of theological seminary. Among the first students at St. Sebald were several who would shortly volunteer for work among the Indians to the West.

*Explorations in Indian Country*

As soon as the new synod was organized Loehe renewed his plea: begin work among the native people of North America. In 1856 a new arrival from Neuendettelsau, Pastor John Jakob Schmidt, was designated Iowa's first missionary to the Indians. To seek a locale for the work, Schmidt with Pastor Sigmund Fritschel of Detroit visited Moraviantown, some 70 miles east of Detroit in Ontario, where they received letters of introduction to the Canadian office for Indian affairs. The government officials advised the Iowans to consider the north shore of Lake Superior. Schmidt visited Grand Portage, at the Ontario-Minnesota border, in the spring of 1857, but learned that the powerful Hudson Bay Company, which controlled the area, favored Roman Catholic mission work. Again there was disappointment in both St. Sebald and Neuendettelsau.

Then came an unexpected stroke of good fortune. In Detroit, through a newspaper story, Schmidt learned that the government's agent for the Crow Indians of Montana, a Mr. A. Redfield, was visiting the city. Schmidt found Redfield, and their conversation led to an invitation to Schmidt to accompany Redfield to the land of the Crows in the spring of 1858. The Crows, Redfield explained, lived generally south of the Yellowstone River and between the Big Horn River in the west and the Powder in the east. Redfield would welcome to his area clergy who were without family and willing to live a primitive life-style.

The willingness of Redfield to support the exploration among the Crows was welcome news in Iowa and in Germany. It was agreed that Schmidt should be accompanied by Moritz Braeuninger, a recent arrival at St. Sebald from Germany. Described as kindly disposed and deeply religious, Braeuninger was completely committed to work among the Indians.

Schmidt left Detroit on May 11, 1858, traveling to St. Louis where he met his fellow missionary, Braeuninger. On Pentecost

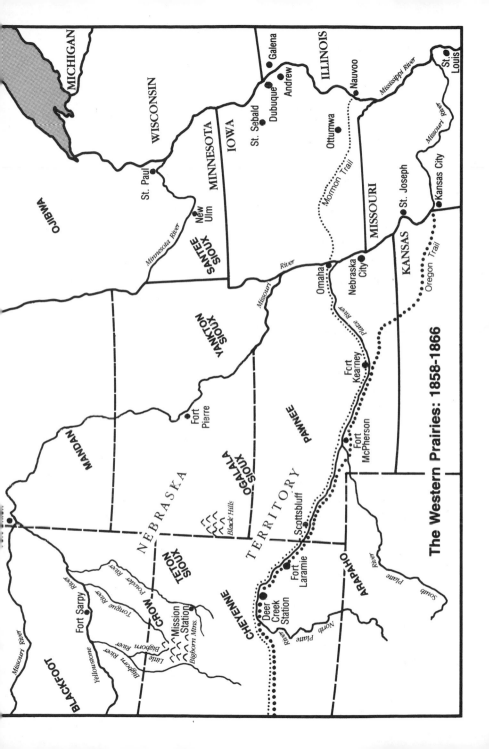

The Western Prairies: 1858-1866

Sunday, May 23, they left St. Louis aboard the government steamer *Twilight,* which would sail up the Missouri to deliver government annuities to the assigned tribes of the Upper Plains in keeping with treaty provisions.

## Broken Treaty

The treaty situation in the Northern Plains was not healthy in the late 1850s and the peace between Indians and whites was, at best, a fragile one. The 1851 Treaty of Fort Laramie sought to assure the Indians of hunting and fishing rights and protection from white encroachment on their designated territories, in exchange for safe passage for whites along the Mormon and Oregon trails, essentially the valley of the North Platte in Nebraska and Wyoming. The Indians whose chiefs signed the treaty—various Sioux or Dakota tribes, Cheyennes, Arapahoes, Crows, Assiniboines, Gros-Ventres, Mandans, and Arriakaras—were promised for 10 years the payment of annuities in the form of provisions, domestic animals, agricultural implements, and other goods.

As soon as the treaty was signed whites began to scoff at it and ignore it. Those traveling westward and those who came to settle in the North Platte valley adopted their own rules and regulations. The Cheyennes and Sioux finally withdrew in anger and resignation from the widely traveled Platte valley, their hatred and sense of futility growing year by year. ''Resistance to white encroachment in every form was the one consistent policy of the Sioux.''[4]

Building roads and forts in Indian country seemed to legitimate the white presence and to invite more of the same. It foreshadowed a drastic change in the Indians' way of life because it restricted them to specific areas and inevitably forced them into either the alien style of sedentary farming or dependence on government handouts.

The Treaty of Fort Laramie failed in its goals, but it succeeded quite well in increasing "the annuity business on the Upper Missouri and threw the American Fur Company and its adversaries into thirteen years of hotter-then-ever competition for the annual government contract."[5] The yearly contract-letting and subsequent delivery of goods at certain times and places along the Missouri and Yellowstone Rivers led to blatant profiteering by certain subcontractors and to growing cynicism among the suffering Indians, as the missionaries were to observe.

By the late 1850s, it was generally agreed that the treaty had brought no lasting peace to the Platte valley and the region northward to the Yellowstone. Dee Brown sums up the developments of the 1850s:

> By the end of the first decade following the treaty the white men had driven a hole through the Indian country along the valley of the Platte River. First came the wagon trains and then a chain of forts; then the stagecoaches and a closer-knit chain of forts; then the pony express riders, followed by the talking wires of the telegraph.[6]

This is the social/political climate into which Schmidt and Braeuninger were traveling in the summer of 1858.

### With the Crows of the Yellowstone

The first stage of the journey, to Fort Union near today's Williston, North Dakota, a trip of nearly 2400 miles, consumed exactly one month. En route, the missionaries spoke often with Redfield, who promised them a license to work among the Crows upon their arrival at Fort Union. Redfield also indicated that they could return the following year (1859) and establish a mission near Fort Union, with probably a school and a farm. Schmidt played also with the idea of going to the Blackfeet and talked about that possibility with an agent for the Blackfeet who was on board.

Fort Union was located at the confluence of the Yellowstone River with the Missouri, at the North Dakota-Montana border. A fur trading center established by the American Fur Company 30 years before, it was a substantial and liveable outpost in the late 1850s, a combination of rude and carefree frontier life-style with imported elegance of eastern civilization. The missionaries spent an unpleasant two weeks at Fort Union. Schmidt writes in his journal:

> Not only did we have to see the crying injustices committed to the Indians but also the changing of the fort to a house of drunks and whores. . . . The pain over it depressed us deeply. We personally had to suffer much.[7]

The experience at Fort Union was an almost overwhelming moral jolt for the two gentle men of God. They were most eager to move on to the yet unspoiled Crows to carry out their mission. They were more than ready to depart on July 7, 1858, for their next destination, Fort Sarpy, some 300 miles upstream on the Yellowstone. It took 37 days to make the trip, their headway slowed by low water, requiring constant cordelling (pulling the boat with rope from the shore by men or horses).

Fort Sarpy (near the site of today's Forsyth, Montana) was, if anything, more depraved than Fort Union. The distribution of annuities to certain Indians was made, but in a way that left the missionaries convinced they were being defrauded. Not all the Indians arrived to claim their goods; the remainder was to be placed in storage for later delivery. At one point Schmidt was invited by Redfield to certify that the goods were properly delivered to the Indians. Schmidt declined, despite his knowledge that honest whites were in short supply at Sarpy, because he felt it would compromise their mission.

### Travel with the Crows

On August 17, the two missionaries made a momentous decision. They asked Dagbizaschusch, a Crow chieftain whom they had come to know and respect at Fort Sarpy, if they could travel and live with his people as they left the fort. The Crow leader readily agreed. The two Iowans thus spent the next six weeks on the move with their Crow friends. They traveled first to the southwest, to the Bighorn River, thence southeast to the Tongue River, through the region where General George Custer would have a final meeting with some other Indians 18 years later, and into what is now Wyoming, along the east face of the Bighorn Mountains. They traveled through the Powder River valley, probably not far from the site Braeuninger would choose for a mission station two years hence. Eventually they found their way with a part of the Crow band to Deer Creek on the North Platte, an Indian agency station near the present town of Glenrock.

While with the Crows, Schmidt and Braeuninger learned the elements of the language, became familiar with Crow culture, and began theological discussions with some of the Indian leaders. They were eager to travel back to Iowa and begin planning for the return to their beloved Crows next summer and the establishment of a permanent mission among them. The Crows were reluctant to see them leave, as Schmidt reported:

> A thousand times they asked us if we would really return when the winter had passed and the grass grew again. Some even offered to accompany us to Iowa, which offer we had to decline.[8]

Leaving Deer Creek in early October, the two journeyed down the Oregon Trail to the Kansas City area, traveling on to St. Louis by boat on the Missouri. They reached St. Sebald at last on Nov. 24, a full half year after their exploratory mission began. They were not expected but were welcomed home with great joy. And the news they brought was positive: there was an open field for them among the Crows. Missionaries, farmers, and goods and equipment were needed for starting up the work in the western prairies.

Euphoria prevailed among the supporters in Iowa, and soon also in Germany. Via a report published in the Nürnberg church paper, *Missionsblatt*, in early 1859, Schmidt offered these conclusions along with an appeal for financial support:

1. The traders (whom Schmidt called "zealous missionaries of the devil") must be removed from the region if missionaries are to accomplish anything. The church itself should provide people to manage honest trade for the Indians.

2. We should set up a farm in a fertile area, with agricultural experts who can teach the Indians how to settle and cultivate the land.

3. A church and a school building should be built, along with houses of log construction. A small colony should be developed, and then additional Lutheran families should be settled there. To build the settlement, Schmidt felt "at least 12 devoted young men are needed."

### The Powder River Station

Despite the high expectations of the previous fall, the actual departure for the West in 1859 suffered both setbacks and cutbacks, because financial support was lacking. It was not until July 5, 1859, that the mission party was able to leave Iowa. The destination was the Deer Creek station on the North Platte in Nebraska Territory (today's Wyoming). The group would include Schmidt, another pastor (Ferdinand Doederlein), the seminarian Theodore Seyler, and two farmers, Beck and Bunge. At the last minute, upon his own insistence, Braeuninger was added to the team.

They took the overland route with heavy, well-equipped wagons, using first horses and then oxen to cross Iowa and into Nebraska. Following the Platte via Kearney and Fort Laramie, they arrived in late fall 1859 at Deer Creek. Most of their supplies and funds were consumed on the long journey. Their major disappointment was the discovery that their beloved Crows were not in the vicinity, nor had they come to Deer Creek in the spring, as agreed. To add to the group's misery, Schmidt, who had been ailing most of the trip, decided to return to Iowa and missionary Doederlein accompanied him. They said they would return early in the spring of 1860 with more men and goods.[9]

The group at Deer Creek, now under Braeuninger's leadership, was almost without financial resources. Fortunately, Captain W. F. Raynolds of the U.S. Army Corps of Engineers, who was wintering at Deer Creek, provided some employment for the mission workers through the long winter, for which they received food, lodging, and some money. They celebrated Christmas by decorating a spruce tree with candles. Captain Raynolds read the Christmas gospel in English and Braeuninger in German. Local Indians were present and one of Raynold's officers explained the meaning of Christmas in the Indian tongue. Captain Raynolds played the flute and Braeuninger the violin to accompany Christmas carols.

Captain Raynolds was eager to help the missionaries to establish their colony. As a government surveyor, he knew the region well and suggested a location ''near the lower canyon of the Bighorn River,'' the heartland of the Crows.[10]

Just after Easter of 1860, the Braeuninger expedition moved northward. Braeuninger thought the location recommended by Raynolds was too far from the next postal station and therefore chose a location on the Powder River, closer to a post office (but still 100 miles away). The site, surrounded by thick grass and many cottonwood trees, offered (they thought) a safe and central location for their work among the Crows. In reality they had chosen the eastern boundary of the Crow territory, adjacent to Sioux tribes that were hostile to the Crows and to whites.

They built a simple loghouse, dug a well for drinking water, plowed the soil and planted vegetables: corn, beans, and melons.

They built a fence for a corral to protect their cattle and a chicken coop. Later they added a cellar and a larger kitchen. Wolves threatened their livestock and chickens. But the land also offered antelope, ducks, and geese to hunt.

After a few weeks of hard work, the group suffered another disappointment. Bunge declared his resignation and desire to return to Iowa. Braeuninger sadly agreed to accompany Bunge to Deer Creek. While there he replenished supplies and prepared a report on the progress made at Powder River, to send back to Iowa with Bunge. He included a sketch of the station.

Then Braeuninger trekked north again to the Powder River station. The three remaining members of the team began to reflect on their future. When would Iowa send more colonists to build a self-supporting mission farm? Would more ordained men be coming to undertake the evangelistic work? Should they fortify their station like a military post for protection? Such thoughts were often in the conversation of the three. But it was still midsummer, the vegetables were growing, and the situation seemed quite tolerable.

Within a month, all was changed. Braeuninger was gone, apparently dead. The station was abandoned. The two survivors, Seyler and Beck, were back at Deer Creek, wondering with newly arrived colleagues Krebs and Flachenecker if the work among the Crows would ever be resumed.

### New Work with the Cheyennes

The loss of Braeuninger was a sad blow to the mission board of the Synod. When they met in early September, they resolved to continue the work in the West, but specified that Deer Creek should become the home base. It was considered safer and was a meeting place for more Indians, including tribes other than Crows. Iowa also voted to send Pastor Christian Kessler to join the four workers at Deer Creek, none of whom was ordained. (It had been expected that Braeuninger would ordain Krebs and Flachenecker.)

Krebs wrote home in October that the four had found a location for their new station a mile and a half from Deer Creek trading post, south of the North Platte River along Deer Creek. They would build there in the spring of 1861. Pastor Kessler arrived early that spring to assume leadership of the mission. He immediately ordained Krebs and Flachenecker.

In May 1861, Kessler, Krebs, and Seyler left Deer Creek looking for Indians. They headed north and seemed drawn to the Powder River location. At the site of the station, now in ashes, they camped for several days. Finding no Indians, they returned to Deer Creek, hoping Indians might be there. Finally in August, Cheyennes came. Flachenecker and Kessler were allowed to travel with them; in four weeks they learned the basics of their language.

During 1862, tensions between whites and Indians were high at all points along the frontier. Civil War fighting back East had led to reduced garrisons at the frontier forts. The uprising of Sioux (Dakota) around New Ulm in southwest Minnesota encouraged Indians elsewhere to take up arms. Many stage stations along the Oregon-Mormon Trail west of Fort Laramie were raided and burned. Flachenecker, Krebs, and Beck moved to the safer Fort Laramie for several weeks in the summer of 1862, while Kessler and Seyler returned to Iowa for supplies; when they journeyed back to Wyoming in the spring of 1863, another seminary graduate, Franz Matter, was with them.

Through most of the years 1861-63, preaching services were held for Indians near the mission station at Deer Creek. Eventually, some of the Cheyennes learned to pray the Lord's Prayer in their own language. When three orphaned Cheyenne boys were entrusted to the missionaries, Krebs especially focused on teaching them the Scriptures, writing, simple mathematics, even the German language! Brown Moccasin, the older of the three, was the quickest to learn. He was baptized on Christmas Day 1863 at Deer Creek. He was christened Sigmund Friedrich, after his sponsor Sigmund Fritschel, a pastor and mission board leader back in Iowa. A second boy was baptized on Easter 1864 and named Paulus, after Paulus Bredow, another Iowa pastor. The third boy was baptized some months later in Galena, Illinois, and named Gottfried, after the second Pastor Fritschel of the Iowa Synod.

By the summer of 1864, a new wave of Indian insurrections was rolling over the Northern Plains, hitting especially the much-traveled trails to the West along the Platte. The demands of the Civil War had reduced army forces to a minimum in the West. The missionaries at Deer Creek were dangerously exposed to attack.

Warnings by friendly Cheyennes in September that an attack on Deer Creek was coming within days led the missionaries again to withdraw to Fort Laramie. They had a divine service together on September 25. Most of them left for Iowa the next day, missionaries Flachenecker and Matter remaining at Fort Laramie. The travelers joined an ox train for safety, but the air they breathed was full of rumors, anxieties, and fear of attacks. Once they reached Fort Kearney, on October 20, they began to feel more secure. From there they continued on to Nebraska City, to Ottumwa, Iowa, north to the synod's new orphanage at Andrew, and then to Dubuque by November's end. The group included Pastor and Mrs. Kessler and child, Mr. and Mrs. Beck and child, Mr. Seyler and Mr. Glaeser, and Pastor Krebs with his three Cheyenne students.

Krebs and the boys went on to Wartburg Seminary at St. Sebald, where Krebs continued their education. Within a year, two of them had died of lung disease. Gottfried succumbed on August 2, 1865, Paulus on December 15. Both are buried in the St. Sebald cemetery. Their grave marker includes a tribute to the memory of Moritz Braeuninger.[11]

Flachenecker and Matter also returned from Fort Laramie in late January 1865. For the first time in more than six years, there were no Iowa Synod missionaries in Wyoming.

### The Work Is Ended

The synod made one more attempt. In the spring of 1866 Krebs, Matter, and Sigmund Friedrich (the one surviving Indian) were commissioned to resume their work at Deer Creek. The trio traveled via Des Moines, Omaha, and the Platte valley in a farm wagon pulled by four mules. At Fort McPherson, just east of North Platte, Nebraska, they had to stop because of war-like conditions ahead. They waited there for eight months, returning to Iowa early in 1867.

Matter and Krebs were told at Wartburg that the mission would not be resumed until the Indians were utterly defeated and transferred permanently to reservations. Matter later observed, "Our mission among the Indians was buried when we left Fort McPherson."

A few months later, at its synod meeting in Toledo, Ohio, the Iowans declared their work among the Indians temporarily suspended, though Krebs was urged to watch for opportunity to resume work with the Cheyennes. It never came. In 1885 the synod formally closed the effort by transferring accumulated Indian mission funds to the Neuendettelsau Mission Society, for its new work on the island of New Guinea. Much of Iowa's own mission energy for the next century would flow to that Pacific land.

What happened to Sigmund Friedrich, the surviving Cheyenne convert? Friedrich, first to be baptized and always the exemplary student, was an agreeable young man while under the guidance of Krebs. But the culture of Iowa was not easy for him to live

with. Reports about him after 1867 are shrouded in mysterious
allusions to temptations and departures from "the paths of righ-
teousness." Zeilinger reports that he too died young and that
"those who knew him believe God's grace helped also this wan-
dering sheep to reach home."[12]

The Powder River station is long forgotten, its exact site unknown today. In 1862, gold was discovered in southwest Montana, and the next year John M. Bozeman pioneered a trail north
from the North Platte into Montana. The Bozeman Trail crossed
the Powder River just a couple miles downstream from the area
where the mission station stood. In 1865, a military post, Fort
Reno, was built where the Bozeman Trail crossed the Powder.
It was abandoned and burned three years later. A monument is
all that marks its location today.

### Conclusion

The critical reader can detect many reasons for the failure of
the Iowa Synod's efforts among the western Indians. One could
blame the involved chain of command from Bavaria via Iowa to
the frontier; the haphazard planning, lack of funds, and inexperience of the synod's mission board; the faulty logistics and exhausting travel routes to the frontier; the inter-tribal conflicts
among the Indians; the dishonesty of many whites with whom
the Indians dealt; the routine violation of treaties by whites in
general; the untimely outbreak of the Civil War and the concom-
itant withdrawals of military forces in the West; and finally the
inexperience, isolation, and naivete of the German-speaking missionaries operating in a twice-foreign environment. The collusion
of all these forces brought about the collapse of the Iowa Synod's
hopeful, visionary enterprise among the Indians of the western
plains.

Still, the effort was in many ways a remarkable one. A people
came across the ocean with the gospel. Even before arriving in
the New World, they had the compelling vision that it must be

shared with the native peoples of their adopted land. Uprooted by a theological dispute they did not desire in one place, they moved on to root themselves in another, carrying the vision with them. Even as they organized a new church, they planned with meager resources to seek native Americans with whom they might live the gospel. When there were too few trained leaders to care for their own people settling in the farmlands of the Midwest, they deployed many of their best for the mission in the West. After disappointments, even the death of one of their top men, they did not quit. For seven more years they stayed with their vision. And when at last they did suspend the effort, the remaining resources were directed to another alien culture, the Papuans of New Guinea, where it would be 13 long years before the first Baptism!

## *A Personal Note*

Author Schmutterer recently made several trips to the locales of the activities recounted in this story in the years 1858 to 1867. He visited the remnants of Fort Union, near Williston, North Dakota; the vicinity of Glenrock, Wyoming, where Deer Creek station was located; and Fort Laramie. Finally, he traveled along the Yellowstone and then undertook a pilgrimage of love in search of the ill-fated mission station on the Powder River between the hamlet of Sussex, Wyoming, and the historic marker for Fort Reno.

Walking through the high grass among the cottonwoods near the muddy Powder River, in the company of the local young rancher, he experienced the eerie loneliness of the Wyoming prairie along with the exhilarating thrill to have walked, very likely, on the spot of Braeuninger's station. He could visualize the Indians of various tribes roaming the banks of the river, hunting the once-abundant buffalo herds. He wished that one of those giant cottonwoods could tell him the exact location of the mission station and recount all the events of the summer of 1860.

Finally, he wished that today's descendants of those pioneer missionaries might find it appropriate to place a historical marker near the Powder River site, or the Deer Creek location, in honor of Moritz Braeuninger and his brave colleagues who worked gallantly among the Indians of Wyoming territory a century and a quarter ago.

United Danish (1884)

# The Prairie Sod Was Hard
## How Shall Personal Faith Commitment Be Nurtured?

by Theodor I. Jensen

It was the final third of the 19th century before Danish-Americans would have their own Lutheran church bodies in the United States. And yet, Christians from Denmark were responsible for some of the earliest European presence in North America:

- In A.D. 1112 Pope Paschal II named a Dane—Erik Upsi (also called Erik Knutson)—as bishop of Greenland and Vinland. Bishop Upsi resided in Greenland and in 1121 made a trip to Vinland—probably Labrador—and is believed to have celebrated Christmas there that year.[1]
- In 1619, a year before the English Pilgrims landed at Plymouth Rock, Jens Munk led a Danish expedition to Hudson Bay, Canada. Most of the 65 men failed to survive the severe winter of 1619-20; when their chaplain, Rasmus Jensen, succumbed on February 20, 1620, he became the first Lutheran pastor to die in North America.[2]
- There was a Danish community in New Amsterdam (New York) in 1633, served by Pastor Christian Pedersen Abel of Aalborg. One of the best known Danes in New Amsterdam, who arrived in 1639, was Jonas Bronck, for whom the Bronx was named.[3]

• The first Lutheran work in the Caribbean was organized by Lauritz Andersen Rhodesius, sent to the Danish Virgin Islands by the Church of Denmark in 1656. The islands were served by Danish pastors until 1917, when Denmark sold them to the United States.

This essay will paint a portrait of one group of Danish Lutherans in the United States, the church body known as the United Evangelical Lutheran Church (UELC) prior to its union in the new American Lutheran Church in 1960. We will focus on the formative years of what became the UELC, approximately 1870 to 1910. Some historical data will be necessary, but this chapter will offer mostly a set of pictures seeking to show who these Danish-Americans were and what made them distinctive.

### 1872: Danes Organize a Church

Danish immigration to the mainland of North America was not numerically large until the 1850s. The first Danish settlement was begun in 1845 at Hartland, Wisconsin. Two years earlier a teacher from Denmark, Claus L. Clausen, had arrived in southeast Wisconsin. This Dane, after ordination at Muskego by a *German*-origin group—the Buffalo Synod (see Chapter 2)—spent his life in ministry among *Norwegian* Lutherans in the Upper Midwest.

The first Danish congregation in what is now The ALC—Emmaus Church of Racine, Wisconsin—was founded in 1851. At first serving Scandinavians generally, within a few decades it became specifically Danish. Dozens of other Danish Lutheran congregations were organized in the next three decades, chiefly in a band reaching from Wisconsin through Iowa to Nebraska.

Before they had their own church bodies, Danes found themselves associated with other Scandinavians, especially Norwegians. That made some sense because, until 1814, Danish kings had been ruling Norway for almost 400 years. The word *Danish* appeared in the names of two groups organized in 1870: the Norwegian-Danish Augustana Synod and the Conference for the Norwegian-Danish Evangelical Lutheran Church in America.

There were no Danish pastors in either, but both groups sought to serve Danes, who were now arriving in large numbers and often settling with Norwegians. The Conference in 1872 said its Norwegian pastors were serving about 20 Danish congregations, and its seminary, Augsburg in Minneapolis, claimed several Danish students.[4]

Finally, in 1872, the Danes in the United States formed the first church body designed explicitly to meet the needs of their own immigrants. Named the Danish Evangelical Lutheran Church (often shortened to "the Danish Church"), it existed as the sole Danish-American Lutheran body for 12 years. In 1884 another group of Danes organized what came to be known as "the Blair Church"—its offices and seminary were in Blair, Nebraska. After 12 more years, the Blair Church joined with a breakaway portion of the 1872 Danish Church—known as "the North Church"—to form the United Danish Evangelical Lutheran Church in America. (In 1945 it streamlined its name to United Evangelical Lutheran Church—UELC.) It is this group, usually referred to as "the United Church," that helped form the ALC in 1960.

Why did *two* Danish churches emerge in the United States, in the same geographic area and among basically the same immigrant people? The answer is that there were two tendencies in Denmark's church life during the latter half of the 19th century. One followed the emphasis of Bishop N. F. S. Grundtvig, a renewer of the Danish church, bishop 1861-75, poet, and author of beloved hymns (eight appear in the *Lutheran Book of Worship*). The other flowed from the movement known as *Indre Mission* (Inner Mission), which focused on the work of evangelism within already established congregations.

At first the two tendencies coexisted within the one U.S. Danish Church, the body organized in 1872 by four pastors at Neenah, Wisconsin. By 1894 the difference had widened into a formal split, one which was never really healed. The Grundtvig-oriented group became part of the Lutheran Church in America in 1962,[5] while the Inner Mission group entered The ALC in 1960. (The new Lutheran church planned for formation in the late 1980s will at last bring together descendants of these two strains of Danes, after more than a century of separation.)

The specific, immediate reason for the 1894 split was disagreement about the Bible as the Word of God. The Inner Mission people accepted the Bible in its totality as the inspired Word; the Danes following Grundtvig regarded the biblical writings as useful for teaching, but insisted that the living word directly from the lips of our Lord, the life-giving word, is the Apostles' Creed and the baptismal covenant.[6]

### The Inner Mission Movement

Inner Mission as a movement in Denmark originated mainly among Christian lay people who were troubled by decline of spiritual life in the Church of Denmark. The church in the 1850s had become impersonal and formalistic. Many of its clergy were little more than government functionaries in the church. To vast numbers of Danes, the church was simply a convenient place to have their children baptized and confirmed, and to have themselves married and buried. Spirituality was in a sad state and most clergy could not be expected to help; they were a part of the problem.

Thus Christian lay people, in tune with the Lutheran doctrine of the priesthood of all believers, banded together with the goal of doing something about the life and health of the Danish church. They dedicated themselves to evangelism in the hope of awakening "sleeping Christians" in the church, as well as bringing others into a living faith relationship with God. The Inner Mission people did not ignore foreign mission. In fact, they built a splendid record in both foreign and social mission activity. But they had dedicated themselves especially to what they felt to be the critical need at their moment in history—to be God's voice calling to the people of Denmark: "Repent and return to God."

Among the Danish immigrants to North America in the closing three decades of the 19th century were many who came from Inner Mission circles in the homeland. It was thus natural that late 19th-century evangelistic work among Danes in America should be marked by Inner Mission characteristics.

## *Lay People Take the Lead*

Nowhere is the Inner Mission stamp more evident than in the evangelism activity of the immigrants. Almost before they had finished unpacking their few belongings, and often before any pastors were available, highly committed lay men and women were at work on the frontier with the gospel, seeking to bolster the faith of their fellow Danes scattered across the prairies. One of these lay people deserves special mention.

His name was Jens Dixen. He worked as a tile digger near Coulter, Iowa, during the decade of the 1880s. He liked to say, "I know how to use a tiling spade." He did indeed, but he also knew how to visit with people about Jesus Christ. And he knew how to preach. Dixen preached a great deal—at evening meetings, on weekends, and during winter months when he could not go tiling. He saved money from his tiling income and gave generously to the work of missions in other lands. He traveled overseas to visit missionary work and attended the 1910 founding session of the International Missionary Conference, a predecessor of the World Council of Churches, in Edinburgh, Scotland.

Dixen also spent several years teaching and administering at Brorson High School, a Danish folk school near Kenmare, North Dakota. Many of the young men who came to Brorson became pastors in the United Church; all testified that Jens Dixen had something to do with their decision to serve the Lord in pastoral ministry. Dixen came to the United States in 1880; from then on he was a dedicated and effective lay evangelist in the United

G. B. Christiansen
1851-1929
first president
United Danish Church

Jens Dixen
1858-1931

Church. When this writer was in his teens he had the singular good fortune of meeting Jens Dixen, a man of God he has not been able to forget.

## Danish Immigrants Are Hard Soil

The early pastors and lay people faced a difficult field for evangelism among the Danes in the United States. There were the physical hardships encountered in reaching the people in distant and widely scattered prairie settlements—in summer heat and winter cold, on foot or, at best, on horseback or with horse and buggy. Always the funds were meager and the workers too few.

But much more challenging than the physical hardships was the seeming barrenness of the field. Missionaries among other Lutheran immigrant groups—Germans, Swedes, Norwegians—faced similar physical hardships. But one wonders whether they found the sod so hard and resistant to the plow as did these missionaries to the Danes who came in the late 19th century.

One of the discouragements was a pervasive indifference to the church and its message among many Danish settlers. True, not a few had been hoping and praying that someone would come to establish the church among them. But these were a minority. President G. B. Christiansen said in his report to the United Church in 1897, "It is a frightening fact that of approximately 250,000 Danes in America only about 60,000 to 65,000 have anything to do with religion."[7]

The majority of the Danes who came to America came to make a living—not to find religious freedom or for other faith-related reasons. Whatever interest they may have had in the church while still in Denmark was for many lost soon after they arrived in the States, occupied as they suddenly were with the full-time toil of domesticating a recalcitrant prairie. And, frankly, many had become indifferent to the church before they left home. Some had become openly hostile to the church, influenced by an anti-Christian atmosphere in Denmark during the latter half of the 19th century. Followers of the popular critic, George Brandes, sharply attacked the Christian faith and the Church of Denmark. Many of the young people who emigrated during the 70s, 80s, and 90s had been under the spell of virulent antichurch utterances and did not respond enthusiastically when evangelists sought them out in the New World.

Another discouraging factor was the serious shortage of ordained pastors. There were outstanding lay leaders, such as Jens Dixen, who stepped into the situation. But there was always a feeling that something important was lacking if there was no ordained pastor to lead. The Church of Denmark for decades showed insufficient interest in sending pastors to North America—and in this respect was markedly different from the Lutheran churches elsewhere in Europe. There were repeated calls to Denmark, especially to the board of the Inner Mission there, to send pastors. Some did come, but always too few and too late.

### Evangelism Methods

The methods used by the United Church in its evangelism were inherited largely unchanged from the Inner Mission in Denmark. There was person-to-person witness concerning the faith. It was regarded as a basic responsibility of every Christian to give personal witness to others. Then there was the weekly house meeting in many congregations, called in Danish *Samtalemøder*, or conversation meetings. The writer recalls accompanying his mother each week to such a meeting. It consisted of prayer, Bible reading, conversation about the reading, and sharing with one another our current struggles and joys of the Christian life. Those attending these conversation meetings probably did not know that Luther spoke of Christian conversation as one of the means of grace, but these small group meetings were indeed vehicles of the grace of God.

And mention must be made of the semiannual three-day *Missionsmøde*, a special evangelistic meeting with one or two, sometimes even three, guest preachers. This "Mission Meeting" came to be almost an institution in the United Church. The church's president often had a paragraph on its importance in his annual report. In one of these, he wrote, "The regular Sunday morning worship services are as it were a gentle, refreshing rain. By comparison . . . the Mission Meeting is a cloudburst of God's blessing upon his church."[8]

Some of these evangelism methods probably overstayed their usefulness; not a few thought so. But in their day they were fruitful of that which was the church's central aim: the strengthening of the faith of God's people and the evangelization of those who were not yet in the household of believers.

The United Church's early concern for the Danish immigrants in North America was not its only evangelistic interest. At its 1897 convention President Christiansen made an emotional appeal to the people not to forget certain other fields which he hoped would be prominent in their prayers and their giving: the American Indians, the Mormons in Utah (many thousands of whom were Danes who had been "deceived by the Mormon lies"), China, Japan, and the Jews.[9] The United Church by 1903, when just a few years old, was engaged in work among Cherokees in Oklahoma, among Danes who had become Mormons in Utah, and in Japan.

### Education as a Priority

Education was regarded as a primary evangelizing tool from the beginning. In their fervor, the immigrants made decisions which to our reasoning minds seem foolhardy, even irresponsible. When the Blair Church was formed in 1884, the organizers (representing 19 small congregations with 9 pastors) formally established a theological seminary. The church early recognized that a seminary was essential if it was to have educated and ordained

Old Main
central section
completed in 1886
Dana College

pastors. Since they could not be expected to come from Denmark or from any other seminary in the United States, it would have to train them itself. The school opened later that same year as Trinity Seminary in Blair, with four students, in the home of its one professor, A. M. Andersen. Within two years its first building—a part of the present Old Main on the Dana College campus—was completed.

From the beginning Trinity had a preseminary department. By the turn of the century it was joined by Elk Horn College from Iowa, and a few years later this junior college in Blair was given the name Dana College. By the early 1920s it had become a four-year institution.

The United Church also understood that the Christian education of children and youth is essential. One of the early champions of this understanding was Pastor Kristian Anker, a teacher by profession in Denmark before he emigrated. He founded a folk high school in Elk Horn, Iowa, similar to those he knew in Denmark, and urged that others be established. Between the late 90s and early years of the 20th century, high schools were opened in Kenmare, North Dakota; Racine, Wisconsin; and Hutchinson, Minnesota. They helped Danish immigrant youth to a knowledge of the Bible and the English language, but financial distress forced them all to close by World War I.

Parish education—on Sundays, Saturdays, and during summer vacations—was also urged upon the congregations. By 1902 it was reported that nearly all congregations had Sunday schools.

## Personal Commitment

Another important Inner Mission legacy to the United Church was its understanding of the Christian faith in relation to God's saving activity in Jesus Christ. The church understood very well the fundamental importance of Baptism as incorporation into the body of Christ. It understood just as well that justification of the sinner is brought about by God's grace.

Yet, preaching in the United Church never tired of pointing out that the baptized individual must at some time in his or her life consciously acknowledge personal sinfulness and the need of God's forgiveness, and accept that grace as one's very own. In other words, there must be something of a transition from an innocent, passively receptive childhood faith to a state of conscious, personal acceptance of what God has done in Christ. This transition carried the connotation of *decision*.

Often this decision-making crisis in a baptized person's life was called "conversion"—an inappropriate term, it seems to this writer, in the case of baptized children of the congregation who had never strayed from their baptismal covenant. The emphasis on decision in relation to baptismal grace is obviously a leaf from the Inner Mission book.

But perhaps there is also some Kierkegaardian influence here. Søren Kierkegaard, Danish religious philosopher and author

(1813-1855), had nothing directly to do with Inner Mission; most of what is written about Inner Mission does not even mention his name. But when one recalls his attack on objective truth unconnected with personal commitment and involvement, whether in philosophy or theology, an attack so substantively akin to the Inner Mission critique of impersonal, formalistic church religion in Denmark, one has to suspect that there was a connection. The United Church was apparently not conscious of Kierkegaard at the time, but his thought may well have been a determining ingredient at several points in what the church thought and did and became.[10]

The writer believes his church was correct in constantly emphasizing that membership in the body of Christ is more than subscription to the creeds and rites of the organized church, that Christian faith, initiated in Baptism, must ultimately issue in conscious, personal commitment to Christ. The United Church did not deviate from this emphasis to the end of its corporate existence. The goal of every element of its evangelism effort was to bring about personal commitment to Jesus Christ on the part of those whom Inner Mission called ''sleeping Christians.'' Parenthetically it should be said that at no time did the United Church limit formal church affiliation to persons who were in this sense committed Christians. If there were actual instances of so-called ''holy congregations'' comprising only the consciously converted, as one recent account has suggested,[11] there is no evidence known to this writer that the church as such understood its emphasis on Christian holiness of life in such a way.

Much as this writer agrees with the emphasis on personal commitment, it is his view that the point was often pressed too hard in the late 19th and early 20th centuries. At times it came close to violating baptismal grace, tending logically to undermine the importance of Christian nurture in the home, the Sunday school, and the confirmation class. It tended also to confuse the youth of the church, who had been baptized and subsequently taught that their Baptism ushered them into the family of believers. For many there was the question, "Am I or am I not a Christian? I have always assumed that I am, but I know nothing of this 'personal commitment' which the pastor and my parents continually speak about." Over the decades, however, as the real purpose of the church's teaching ministry became better understood, the concept of a personal commitment to Christ took on a more healthy, biblical meaning.

## The Ways of the World

One of the main themes in the typical United Church sermon, thus, was the call to repentance and faith in the gospel. A second theme, virtually as important as the first, was a call to holiness of life before God. Such holiness, it was maintained, is the natural fruit, the spontaneous expression of faith. Holiness implies a break with the world and its ways. Did not the apostle Paul say, "What fellowship has light with darkness? . . . Therefore, come out from them, and be separate from them, says the Lord, and touch nothing unclean" (2 Cor. 6:14-17)?

The Inner Mission in Denmark had a word for this break with the world: *Skellet*. It is not easily translated, but it stands in this connection for a distinct, definitive line of separation between the Christian and the unbeliever, or between the believer and "the devil and all his works and all his ways." The word itself was not used much in the United Church, but the idea of a break or dividing line between Christian and world was much in evidence. The line of separation carried a double connotation: renunciation of the world and its ways and commitment to a life that is consistent with one's confession of faith.

The strong insistence on holiness of life was appropriate. It rests on the assumption that there is no room in the Christian's life for values and behavior which characterize our old nature, "the world," in contrast with the values and ways of living which fit the Kingdom of God. Still, there was a preoccupation with a definition of holiness which the writer believes was unsound and which probably did some harm. "The world and its ways" was often understood too simply as outward acts or pleasures which, in advance, had been judged harmful or at least not beneficial to the life of the Christian.

It was, for example, quite commonly held that a Christian, almost by definition, does not attend the theatre, does not touch playing cards or liquor, is never seen on the dance floor. And, of course, the pastor and his wife could not risk ever being identified with any of these activities, lest the integrity of their calling and possibly their faith as well be questioned. There was a tendency too simply to judge the genuineness of a person's faith by his or her external life-style—in highly individualistic terms. Little heed, for instance, was given to the Bible's admonitions concerning a break with the world's ways in the realm of economics, or with the world's attitudes toward conflict between the races or the nations.

In a country parish of which the writer was a member many years ago the parishioners on their way to church one Sunday morning were spiritually scandalized when they saw the Sunday school superintendent in his field harvesting wheat. From that day, his Christian faith was considered doubtful, not because he had failed to be at his Sunday school post but because he had done something no true Christian does on a Sunday morning. The extenuating circumstance that rust had gotten into his wheat and that it was therefore critically important to harvest at the earliest possible time was not weighed in the judgment that he had violated his faith. And the farmer himself, a confessing Christian, undoubtedly sat on his harvester that morning with a tormented conscience.

The original evangelical intent of the dividing line concept was valid. It underscored the undeniable fact that the believer and the unbeliever are citizens of two radically different kingdoms and render allegiance to two irreconcilable lordships. In fact, however, the line was often drawn, not between faith and unbelief, but according to certain external behavior patterns which had little to do, for example, with the call to love one's neighbor. And such use of the dividing line invited the presumption to define and make visible the boundaries of the church, which God, who "knows those who are his" (2 Tim. 2:19) has reserved for himself.

This kind of emphasis on separation from "the world and its ways" had another unfortunate result. It tended to create suspicion about all things that are not obviously and directly related to the Christian faith, failing to appreciate the basic goodness of all that God has created for us to enjoy and use. This failure to appreciate God's world in its rich natural and cultural wholeness inevitably led to a rather lean conception of the Christian life. Thus it was with some justification that the United Church people were sometimes nicknamed the "sad Danes" or "holy Danes." The other Danish Lutherans in the United States, those in the Grundtvig tradition, had a brighter and no doubt more wholesome appreciation of God's entire creation.

### Theology in the United Church

Persons outside the United Church often asked about its theology. If "theology" means formal, scholarly research and writing, the United Church indeed made little contribution to theological thought. The visible evidence of noted theologians, position papers, and doctrinal debates is so scarce that one could wonder if the United Church cared much about matters theological.

It has been suggested that there was, in fact, a certain theological indifference in the United Church. If indeed there was such indifference, there were probably two chief reasons. First, the Inner Mission in Denmark, from which the United Church inherited so much, had little interest in theological scholarship as such. It believed that it existed for one purpose only: to preach the gospel to "sleeping Christians" and all others who had not been gripped by its message. The Danish pastors and concerned lay people who had just arrived on the American scene believed they had more important irons in the fire than "doing theology." Their one great passion—to bring the gospel to their countrymen who were scattered like sheep with no shepherd on the far-flung prairies—crowded everything else out of their minds and hearts. The implementation of that passion consumed their time and physical resources so completely that there was literally nothing left for scholarly theological thinking and writing.

Secondly, among the very few ordained pastors on the scene—some from Denmark, the rest from theological seminaries in the United States—very few had any advanced theological training. There was, in the early decades, virtually no scholarly leadership that could give the United Church credible stature in the world of theological thought.

A notable exception was Dr. P. S. Vig, professor in the church's theological seminary, Trinity in Blair, Nebraska. From 1896 until 1928—with the exception of half a dozen years when he returned to parish pastorates—Vig was the church's premier teacher of theology. Earlier he had taught at the seminary of the Danish Evangelical Lutheran Church in West Denmark, Wisconsin (1888-1893) and in the theological department of the folk high school at Elkhorn, Iowa (1894-96). Vig had the qualifications for leadership in theological research, but very little opportunity to exercise them. He was overloaded with teaching and administrative responsibilities, plus numerous auxiliary tasks. (Vig became, for example, a primary writer on Danish immigration history.)

P. S. Vig
1854-1929

If there *was* an element of indifference to formal theology among the Danes in America, that too was likely inherited from the Church of Denmark. By comparison with her European neighbors, Denmark never had much appetite for theological debate. The Danish church has been content with a somewhat more slender formal confessional basis than that which prevails in other Lutheran churches: the three ecumenical creeds of the early church, the Unaltered Augsburg Confession, and Luther's Small Catechism. Its attitude, more implied than stated, has been: "These few basic statements of faith have served us well in the past. Why add further statements, the explication and defense of which might easily disturb the tranquility we now enjoy under the doctrinal statements which continue to serve us well?"

This rather casual confessional stance is somewhat characteristic of the theological atmosphere in the United Church. There was never any question about its confessional basis—it was precisely the same as that of the mother church in Denmark. It confessed its faith as set forth in the confessional writings but was never greatly concerned with finely honed theological nuances. In fact, there was a tendency to regard theological explanations as an intrusion into the sacred precincts of faith and worship.

The rubrics in the Holy Communion liturgy, for example, as received from Denmark and used for many years in the United Church, direct the pastor to say while distributing the elements, "This is the true body of Christ" and "This is the true blood of Christ." Eventually, following the lead of the Church of Denmark, the adjective "true" was removed. The reasoning was that "*true* body" and "*true* blood" are theologically loaded terms and that the communion table is no place to "do theology." It is the place where the believer communes with the Lord, and it is violated if used as an occasion to underscore that we, in contrast to some other churches, do indeed believe in the doctrine of the real presence.

### No Question about the Bible

There may be an element of truth in the charge that, in some respects, the United Church moved too close to the fringes of good Lutheran theology. One of the other Lutheran bodies held that opinion.[12] Was there perhaps a slight semi-Pelagian taint in its strong emphasis on the necessity of the individual's response to, and acceptance of, God's redemptive work? Did it understand Christian living too simply in legalistic, personal-ethical terms? Perhaps.

However, the writer believes that, whatever substance there may have been in these suspicions, it was not doctrinal error as such but a matter of overemphasizing fundamental biblical teachings. It can be said unequivocally that the church wanted to be true to Lutheran confessional teaching in every respect. The United Church president said to the 1899 annual convention: "It is my firm conviction that our future as a church in America depends upon our remaining immovably true to the precious fundamental principles of the Lutheran Church. . . . It is my hope that our seminary may be able to train and send out men who are true sons of the Lutheran church.''[13]

And then there was ''The Professor,'' Dr. P. S. Vig, respected theologian and for three decades teacher at Trinity Seminary in Blair. He knew what genuine Lutheran theology is and he was not slow to speak up when trends in the church deviated from it even only a few degrees. In 1905 he asked if the United Church was so poor that it needed ''the rags of Methodism'' to clothe itself—referring to a reliance on an emotional revivalism.[14] Among the many things for which the United Church is indebted to Dr. Vig is his having guided it on a course between an un-Lutheran subjectivism and an equally un-Lutheran formalistic orthodoxy.

The Bible was held to be unqualifiedly the Word of God. There had been disagreement among U.S. Danish Lutherans on that point. Stated too simply, the issue was whether the Bible *is* the Word of God or *contains* the Word of God. This disagreement was a large factor in the split in the Danish Church in 1894 and the subsequent formation of the United Church in 1896. In the United Church there was always unanimity on the acceptance of the Bible as the divinely inspired Word of God. It was an acceptance which did not occupy itself with explanations of how the words on the page can be God's voice to human beings. The doctrine of scriptural inspiration was never a matter of serious discussion, either in congregations or in national or district conventions.

There were exceptions, to be sure. The writer recalls a Sunday evening when his pastor preached a sermon under the title ''Twenty Reasons Why the Bible Is the Word of God.'' Even to his young ears (the writer was in his teens) this sermon had a strange, offbeat sound. Was not the preacher laboring to prove something which all of us had always assumed to be true?

## Church Consciousness

It has also been said that there was very little consciousness of the larger church—its unity, its universality, its apostolic character—in the United Church. There were certainly factors in the early years which were anything but conducive to the development of church consciousness. The rugged pioneer circumstances of the time did not feed consciousness of anything beyond the immediate, the small, cramped world of a pioneer congregation. There were few ordained clergy, sometimes none, and lay people had to initiate and carry forward the work of evangelism as best they could.[15] Resources were meager, facilities crude—all so different from what the people had been accustomed to think of as the church.

And yet, there was from the beginning more than a little sound, evangelical sense of the church. Back in the log cabin and sod house days there was, for instance, serious talk about whether the church should have a bishop.[16] There were some who strongly supported the idea. But after several years of intermittent discussion, the idea was laid to rest. An attempt to revive the bishop idea was made by a few enthusiasts every 25 years or so. Thus, episcopacy remained as a subconscious, recessive strain, surfacing here and there in much of United Church history.

Instead of a bishop, the church created a president's office— and proceeded to endow its occupant with as much honor and almost as much power as would be accorded any bishop. He was the church's ordainer. He had the prerogative of speaking for the church. And his voice weighed heavily in almost any discussion of church policy or direction.

Further, there was in the United Church something called order, a sense of what is right and proper and what is not. This sense of order was evident in liturgical practice and in virtually everything related to the church's life. There was no high church liturgical fastidiousness; United Church people would have none of that. It was rather a "place for everything and everything in its place" kind of order. Pastors and lay delegates sat together at the church's annual conventions. But at a certain point the convention divided itself into two "houses." There were matters which the laity wanted to discuss among themselves, unencumbered by clergy presence and participation. And the "house" of the clergy, called the ministerium, withdrew to a meeting of its own. The ministerium had a strong voice in the approval of candidates for ordination. It disciplined its own members. It dealt with whatever matters were considered appropriate only for clergy deliberation and decision.

From time to time there were itinerant lay evangelists; they did not travel free-lance, however, but as recognized, certified servants of the church. The rather prominent role of the laity in the evangelism and administrative arms of the church never developed into something outside the church but remained integral to the total life and work of the church.[17]

These are some pictures, some impressions, of the early days of the Danish-Americans who created the United Evangelical Lutheran Church. There is one more picture to be shared, however, before closing this chapter.

The year is 1948. June 17. The UELC in convention at Fresno, California, adopts a resolution inviting the member churches of the American Lutheran Conference to begin discussions toward "an eventual merger of the bodies of the American Lutheran Conference and the other Lutheran bodies of the land."

As a direct result of that invitation, negotiations began which led to the formation of The American Lutheran Church 12 years later. The United Church, half a century old, was ready to give up its Danish identity for the sake of a broader unity in the gospel.

United Norwegian (1890)

# A Church and a College for the World

## Can the Church Be United for Mission?

### by Todd W. Nichol

It is not a moment drenched in drama when the general convention of The American Lutheran Church adjourns for a few minutes, as it always does, to reconstitute itself as the corporation of St. Olaf College. The galleries do not fill, the leaders of the church do not huddle, delegates do not rise to speak one after another, and the sage do not speculate. Nothing hangs in the balance. Dispensing with the item of St. Olaf College is a matter of routine, a mere formality.

It was not always so.

But that is to get ahead of a story beginning elsewhere.

### Emigrants and Immigrants

Immigrants are also emigrants. They are people who decide to leave home. They are women and men who must choose what to take with them into the future. That is how it was for many when Norway hemorrhaged in the 19th century and thousands upon thousands of its people spilled out of a restless and hungry land and into the United States.[1] They came, most of them, in search of food and work and land and money. Some came for elbow room or for a chance to think new thoughts.

Only a few Norwegians left home and came to America for the sake of religion. But their number is deceiving. It is deceptive because all the emigrants, one by one, had to reckon with religion. They had to choose whether to take it with them or not. Many did and many did not. Those who did packed their religion as seemed best to them and as it fit with the rest of their baggage. Some of it they left behind, some of it they discarded as they traveled, and some of it they remade when it ceased to fit. Emigrating was a good rehearsal for America and especially for being religious in America.

The Norwegians fit America well when they arrived. They were, to begin with, white. No bars were to be set in front of them on account of race. Unlike some others who came, they were from the beginning free to seek their own ends. And their purposes suited America's own. Planned by its founders to be a large, commercial republic in which the opportunity to pursue wealth would unite a diverse and factious population, America must have seemed as if it had been made for the hungry, ambitious, and generally industrious Norwegians.[2] Because their race and their purposes fit America so well, the Norwegians assimilated easily into the nation's political structures, most often joining one of the two principal political parties.

But what of religion? The Irish, for example, were white, they adapted instantly and effectively to American politics, and the Erie Canal is a monument to their willingness to work. Nevertheless it took them several generations to fit America as well as the Norwegians were able to do after only one or two. The Irish were, of course, usually city folk and the Norwegians tended to settle down and mind their own business in the calmer countryside and small towns. But there was a more important difference. The Irish were Roman Catholics and the Norwegians were Protestants. Their language, a thing or two about their liturgical practices, a moral peccadillo here and there (even the most devout among them were known to use alcohol and some of them to picnic on Sundays) may have marked the Norwegians as a little odd, but they were indisputably Protestant.

By birthright of race and religion the Norwegians conformed to patterns acceptable to the Americans who owned the banks, taught in the schools, preached in the churches, and sat in the seats of government. Peculiarities were ironed out quickly, and the Norwegians became known, along with other Scandinavians, as excellent "Americanizers." Before long little but language and vestiges of cultural custom remained to identify them as Norwegians. Assimilation was hastened by the choice made by the preponderant majority to send their children to the public schools, the temples of an unofficial and informal, but palpable pan-Protestant religious establishment. All this meant that the Norwegians would find a welcome, even if a sometimes condescending and slightly reluctant one, among the white Protestants who dominated the economic, cultural, religious, and political life of America in the 19th and early 20th centuries.

The Norwegians would not have to endure the troubles that Roman Catholics, Mormons, and some Protestants of a radical stripe have had to face. But America still put to them questions of religion. What had they brought with them and what were they going to make of it?

### *Norwegians Form Denominations*

The questions were not easy. Most of them had inherited a religion which—as religions will do—seemed to have been there time out of mind. In Norway they had lived in a densely textured Lutheranism with an old and comfortable feel to it.[3] It was a religion that one could inherit and nurture: a confessional, familial, tribal, national tradition. Preaching, the liturgy of the Lord's Supper, and the Catechism were the religious stays of a way of life.

Most, but not all, Norwegians found the Lutheranism of Norway comfortable. Some said that it was altogether too comfortable. They were the revivalists and awakeners of the church in 19th-century Norway who inherited the traditions of the lay preacher Hans Nielsen Hauge and his friends (see Chapter 3). Those who followed in Hauge's footsteps thought Christ's flock in Norway was scattered, bewildered, and sleepy. They blamed the shepherds of the flock, the bishops and pastors of the Church of Norway, for not tending to their proper tasks. The Haugeans preached conversion and renewal. They were severe with the church. Yet even these restless spirits remained within the fold. They depended, most of them, on a place there.

But America had no church for them, neither for those who liked the roomy old Church of Norway as it was, nor for those who wanted to awaken, revive, and reshape it. For many, a vast number, America was a moment to depart from membership in the visible Christian church. They simply abandoned it. Others— Norwegian Quakers, Baptists, Methodists, and more—free at last from the coercive measures of the Norwegian state and church, went their own ways.

The Lutherans, now become Norwegian-American Lutherans, sized up America quickly and astutely. Rather than attempting to recreate the Church of Norway on American soil—a possibility none of them seems to have contemplated and that none attempted—they followed a pattern borrowed from their American neighbors. They split into several contending factions and formed distinct denominations, sometimes called "synods" and sometimes "churches," but always cut on the same American pattern.[4]

The Norwegian-American Lutherans understood intuitively and quickly that in America a religion is something you choose. They learned that the controlling impulses in the American experience are what the framers of the American regime predicted and expected they would be: competitive and democratic. As in everything else, there was in the America of the time a free market in religion. A laissez faire denominationalism set the terms of competition and the price of survival. Although the coinage is contemporary, it is not anachronistic to say that the first generations of Norwegian-American Lutherans intuitively mastered, even if they did not fully endorse, the implications of that peculiarly American turn of phrase, "shopping for a church." Further, the Norwegian-Americans were quick to realize that Americans, both natives and immigrants, early learn to decide important things for themselves. In America, they came to understand, you are free to choose a religion, voting as you please with your membership in a denomination or abstaining if you like.

From the resources of its history—its pattern of convictions, ideas, personalities, and experiences—each group elaborated a rationale for a separate existence and appealed to the constituency for its votes. Each had its own ideas about what of the Norwegian inheritance to preserve and each fashioned its own program for building a truly Lutheran church in America. The result was a plethora of American denominations descended from one Norwegian parent, a welter of conflicting loyalties, and a complicated history of ecclesiastical war and peace.

*Two Ends . . .*

Norwegians began arriving in America in 1825, but the Lutherans among them did not begin organizing permanent congregations and denominations until 1843.[5] First to enter the arena of denominational competition was Elling Eielsen, a zealous layman who organized groups of Haugean believers into congregations and the congregations into the Evangelical Lutheran Church in America in 1846 (Chapter 3). Usually referred to as "Eielsen's Synod," this group was marked by a fervently cultivated experiential piety, strong lay leadership, moral rigorism, and "low church" worship. In 1875-76, a majority of Eielsen's Synod withdrew to form Hauge's Evangelical Lutheran Synod in America. The Haugeans were not long alone on the American scene. In

1853 a group of lay delegates from scattered congregations and a small but able cadre of pastors trained by the theological faculty of Norway's university established the Norwegian Evangelical Lutheran Church, the "Norwegian Synod," as it came to be known (see Chapter 5). Their venture was a creative one from the start. Appropriating from Norway only what they thought proper to a truly Lutheran, strictly confessional church, they set out to exemplify a doctrinally pure Lutheranism in the new land. They soon found congenial spirits among Lutherans of the Missouri Synod and struck alliances with them. The Missourians lent the Norwegians aid, even training their pastors for a time, but also drew them into a maelstrom of controversy, the effects of which are felt to the present. The laity and pastors of the Norwegian Synod built a strong, vibrant denomination. They were devoted to the study and elaboration of a highly refined scholastic theology they shared with the Missourians, to some of the traditional liturgical practices of the Church of Norway, and to the extension of the church.

The Haugeans marked one end of the Norwegian-American Lutheran spectrum and the Norwegian Synod the other. By 1870 some other Norwegian-American Lutherans were filling in the space between. In Norway you could choose the established church or you could dissent. In America you could multiply churches. If, on the one hand, you suspected the Haugeans of sectarianism or a pietism gone to seed, or if, on the other hand, you suspected the Norwegian Synod of clerical authoritarianism or orthodoxy turned to the worship of orthodoxy, you could choose to go elsewhere. The result: denominations in search of a middle way.

### . . . And a Middle

Two denominations were formed in 1870 when some Norwegian-Americans withdrew in friendly fashion from the strongly Swedish-American body, the Scandinavian Augustana Synod.

One of the withdrawing groups, the Norwegian Augustana Synod, had absorbed strains of American Protestant pietism and adapted them to Norwegian-American use. It pioneered paths of ecumenical contact, although little came of its efforts. It also emphasized lay participation in the work and worship of the church. This group remained very small during its life of 20 years and did not greatly influence events to come.

It was otherwise with The Conference for the Norwegian-Danish Evangelical Lutheran Church. In the same 20 years "the Conference," as it was called, developed a vital and viable tradition. Its leaders attempted to build a church that would avoid the sectarian extremes they feared latent in Haugeanism and the clerical authoritarianism and Missourian theology they thought they detected in the Norwegian Synod. They envisioned a church embracing a way of life and thought, work and worship, inclusive and flexible enough to allow objective and subjective elements to meet and mingle. It was an ambitious program. Boldly conceived and undertaken as it was, it guaranteed that the Conference would be a hothouse for controversy.

### New School, Old School

It early became apparent that there would, in fact, be a pronounced division of opinion and eventually of loyalties in the Conference.

On one side there ranged the proponents of an imaginative approach to church life in America associated with Augsburg Seminary and led by the brilliant Georg Sverdrup and the doughty Sven Oftedal (see Chapter 9). Sverdrup, Oftedal, and their allies constituted what came to be known as the "New School." They called it "New" because their contribution was regarded as an intrusive novelty by their more conventional colleagues of the so-called "Old School." It was Oftedal who pressed the controversy into the open in 1874 when he published a slashing attack on a theology and practice he regarded as Missourian.[6]

There were three planks in the informal platform of the New School. (1) The adherents of the New School, whose leaders included some of the most skilled theologians ever to appear on the Norwegian-American scene, conceived of theology as an essentially catechetical enterprise. They saw the theology of their opponents as a Missourian scholasticism intent on pickling the truth into thesis after thesis. They preferred to think of theology as a free and living exposition of catechism and Scripture with an eye to context in church and community. (2) Their conception of theology fit their notion of the church. To members of the New School, the individual congregation, the "free and living congregation," as it was often called, represented the heart of the church. Other institutional aspects of the church's life were to be done away with as far as possible. Only such schools and other structures as were absolutely necessary for the life of congregations were to be maintained. America, in their judgment, provided the best opportunity seen by Christians since apostolic times to experiment with the possibilities of a genuinely "free" church. (3) One institution beyond the individual congregations reckoned indispensable by New School partisans was Augsburg Seminary (envisioned as including a preparatory school and a college department). The mastermind of the Augsburg program was Georg Sverdrup, who proposed a highly integrated program of humane and theological studies, all intended to serve the principle of a *menighedsmaessig-presteuddanelse*, a pregnant Norwegian phrase that might be paraphrased as "the education of pastors in conformity with the nature and spirit of a free, living congregation."[7]

The adherents of the Old School, although united with Sverdrup and his allies in opposition to Missourian scholasticism, feared that the Augsburg professors' approach would result in a vague and diffuse theology. The Old School was further reserved about the New School's notion of the church. It blurred the crucial center of the church's life in Word and sacrament, the Old School contended, and it did not properly connect the priesthood of all believers and the pastoral office. Finally, the partisans of the Old School did not share the New School's devotion to the program and cause of Augsburg Seminary.[8]

### Grace Alone and Faith Alone

Meanwhile, yet another denomination appeared on the already cluttered horizon.

The Norwegian Synod found itself entangled in a convulsive struggle over one of the deepest and most difficult of Christian notions: election to salvation. The controversy, as one historian puts it,

> . . . had to do with the relation of grace to faith in effecting the redemption of sinful human persons. Lutheran theology had traditionally emphasized the necessity of both—of grace alone and faith alone. And both sides in the various stages of the controversy continued to insist that grace *and* faith were both necessary. The differences between them had to do with the way in which the terms were to be understood: e.g., does the human person have any responsibility in responding to the initiative of grace? If so, how is one to understand *sola gratia*? If not, how is one to understand the nature of faith?[9]

To put the matter bluntly, and for a moment to chop through important theological subtleties, the questions at stake were: ''What of grace, if salvation is by faith alone?'' *and* ''What of faith, if salvation is by grace alone?'' The controverted questions were often misunderstood in the congregations. There the questions were sometimes caricatured. Who, it was sometimes asked, elects whom? Does God choose people? Or do people choose God?

Two theological parties emerged. One side argued that God in his good pleasure simply elects people ''unto faith.'' They cited

Article 11 of the Formula of Concord in support of their position; taking their stance on this, the "first form" of election traditionally taught by Lutherans, the "first formers" were also called "Missourians," since their position was widely held in the Missouri Synod and events in that church had sparked the controversy. The other side embraced the "second form" taught by the Lutheran dogmaticians of the 17th century and in the widely used *Explanation of Luther's Small Catechism* by the Norwegian Bishop Erik Pontoppidan. They argued that God elects people unto salvation *intuitu fidei*, that is, "in view of the faith" he knows they will one day have. The "second formers" were also called "Anti-Missourians." The course of the controversy—it boiled for decades—has been chronicled elsewhere. It was finally settled among the Norwegian-Americans in 1912 with The Madison Agreement or *Opgjør*, acknowledging both forms as authentically Lutheran alternatives.[10]

The election controversy as it was worked out in the labyrinthine arguments of bold and wrathful theologians, and even more as it was popularly perceived, was an index to the changing nature of Norwegian-American Lutheranism. Election to salvation was never publicly controversial among European Lutherans after the Reformation. It was, however, a question bound to surface in America. In America the Norwegians experienced democracy and a dizzying sense of freedom. The experience altered them and their religion permanently. A Norwegian-American novelist and pundit put this telling conversation in the mouths of three of his characters, two old farmers (Thrond and Søren) and a young pastor (Halvor).

"On which side are you, Thrond?"
"Well, I s'pose I'll have to be on the same side as Gunhild; she knows all about such things. . . . I guess they call it Missouri or Mississippi. . . ."
"Are you having the same trouble here, Halvor?" asked Søren.

"No, it is still quite peaceful here. . . . There is just one woman who bothers me a little. She comes and complains about her husband. She weeps and says, 'You see, Lasse, he is a Missourian, you see; and so he says that if he only does not commit suicide, then it is the Lord who is 'sponsebel for what happens to him. . . . ' "

"What is your opinion, Halvor, about this question of election?"

"Oh, to tell the truth I'm not lying awake nights thinking about it. But I believe . . . that one cannot expect to be elected if one refuses to be a candidate."[11]

The *Opgjør* was a reckoning with important American notions as well as with a question of dogmatic theology.

### Anti-Missourians Organize

Because the election controversy occurred in America, it was almost inevitable that one of its results would be the creation of a new denomination. It happened.

In 1887 a large number of the clergy and congregations advocating the second form of election against the Missourian first form split from the Norwegian Synod. They called themselves the Anti-Missourian Brotherhood and operated for a time as a separate denomination, although they conceived of themselves as a movement dedicated to the pursuit of unity among Norwegian-American Lutherans. Working out their fate as a temporary denomination, even if unwillingly, the Anti-Missourians began to tend to denominational business. Among their tasks was to educate pastors. They chose to locate their seminary at St. Olaf's School, an academy in Northfield, Minnesota, begun by a Synod pastor turned Anti-Missourian, Bernt Julius Muus. During the time the Anti-Missourian seminary was at St. Olaf, the school developed into a college.

A movement and a school thus found one another in 1886-90, and a competitor to Augsburg Seminary appeared on the scene.

## Uniting the Church

By the end of the 1880s three groups stood on the middle ground between the Haugeans on one side and the Norwegian Synod on the other. The three were: the Norwegian Augustana Synod, the Conference, and the Anti-Missourian Brotherhood. Despite the tensions between the Old and New Schools in the Conference, and in spite of the pitched battle raging between the Anti-Missourians and their former colleagues of the Norwegian Synod, a protracted series of delicate negotiations succeeded in bringing the three groups together in 1890 as the United Norwegian Lutheran Church in America. It was a moment of rejoicing on June 13 of that year when Norwegian-American Lutherans began to overcome their fractiousness and move toward unity. An observer described the worship that day in Minneapolis:

At ten o'clock, Friday forenoon, preparations were made at the Conference church [Trinity Lutheran near the Augsburg College campus] for the coming of the other groups. . . . By sitting closely together in and between the pews in the commodious church, about half of the forward part of the church remained empty. And soon the Anti-Missourians began to arrive. When they entered the church they were greeted by the standing assembly with the hymn. . . . "God's Word Is Our Great Heritage." . . . After a short moment of waiting members of the Augustana Synod began to enter, and they were greeted with the first stanza of "Praise to Thee and Adoration."

More than 2000 people . . . now filled the church from altar to door, and this assembly sang . . . "Thee God We Praise." . . . And who at that moment could not help but see, not only ourselves and our children, who down through the ages and generations should walk united upon their way to church, but also that greater gathering when the hosts of the Lord's Church would meet from east and west, from north and from south, around the throne of His glory. And I suppose we should not have been ashamed to

B. J. Muus
1832-1900
leader of
Anti-Missourians

Old Main
St. Olaf
College
ca. 1881

have shed the tears of repentance and humility, joy and gratitude at that moment. . . .[12]

How to assess the church that came into existence that summer day? It had no one animating personality, no single theology, no set of guiding principles, no recognizable way of life that could not be seen elsewhere, not even an approximate uniformity of liturgical practice. The United Church had, in fact, come in American circumstances to reflect the capacious hospitality of the old parent, the Church of Norway. It was inclusive in outlook. Its distinctly American character was manifest in its devotion to mission. It intended to gather as many Norwegian-Americans into itself as would come, and it took preliminary steps toward reckoning with a permanent stay in an America in which its people would one day cease to be hyphenates. It worked to take the gospel to as much of the world as would hear it. And finally, it sought to further unity among the warring Norwegian-American Lutheran synods.

But we are again ahead of the story.

### Controversy over Colleges

Immediately after the union the United Church was torn by bitter controversy. At stake were Augsburg Seminary and St. Olaf College.

The new church asked Augsburg to serve as its seminary and St. Olaf as its college. The decision was unacceptable to the New School proponents of Augsburg. They regarded the adoption of St. Olaf as a threat to their integrated program of studies and to the survival of their school. Galleries filled at the church's conventions, leaders conferred, delegates rose to speak, and the savvy counted heads as the storm broke. After an extended struggle that included theological debate, bitter invective, fighting on convention floors, lockouts, legal maneuvering, and court battles, the result of the controversy was a parting of the ways.

In 1893 the New School's "Friends of Augsburg" departed

from the United Church and in 1897 they formed a separate body, the Lutheran Free Church (see Chapter 9).[13] St. Olaf remained the college of the United Church and the church also went on to establish a new seminary in Minneapolis.

## The Adopted College

It is perhaps in the college it adopted that the nature of the United Church can be seen best.[14] St. Olaf was, in the first instance, a liberal arts college "plain and simple," as it was once put.[15] Its curriculum was for the most part like that of other American schools of its kind, and its course of studies changed over the decades as did theirs. It was not, as were some of the other Norwegian-American colleges and many other American Protestant schools, primarily intended to prepare future pastors for theological study. Nor was it, as were many institutions like it, a school only for males. From the beginning and in face of hostile opposition, St. Olaf offered an education for both women and men.

There were other distinguishing marks. In its early years it was a school specifically intended to serve the young people of the Norwegian-American Lutheran churches. It therefore took up the task of paying attention to what was on both sides of the hyphen. The Norwegian language and literature were studied assiduously and unapologetically, but English was from the very beginning the principal language of the school. The intent was to help Norwegian-American students come to terms, quite literally in the beginning, with the context in which they lived. In some quarters of its constituency St. Olaf was attacked for its aggressively American character. Thorbjørn Nelson Mohn, president of the college in the formative years 1875-1899, was particularly suspect in some quarters for his defense of the school's engagement with context and culture.

T. N. Mohn
first president of
St. Olaf College
1844-1899

Yet it was not these things that most marked St. Olaf as different. What distinguished it from other schools was the guiding conviction that what is good and true and beautiful, what the arts pursue and the sciences search out, is intimately bound up with the gospel of Jesus Christ. To put it another way, St. Olaf intended from the beginning to be a college "plain and simple" *and* a Christian school. Mohn put the connection this way· "It is a noble work to lead man to truth, but it is more noble to lead him beyond it to its source—the God of truth; for God is love, and man is blessed only when in communion with his creator."[16]

Lest the subtlety of the argument, rooted as it is in the First Article of Christian faith, slip by, another remark of Mohn's deserves quotation: "Our school is not what is called a 'school of religion,' yet it is for the sake of religion that this school was founded."[17] It was, indeed, for the sake of a very particular religious tradition that St. Olaf was founded. The purposes of the school were set out in its original articles of incorporation. St. Olaf was founded to

> . . . preserve the pupils in the true Christian faith as taught by the Evangelical Lutheran Church and nothing taught in contravention with the Symbolum Apostolicum, Nicenum & Athanasianum; the Unaltered Confession delivered to the Emperor Charles the Fifth at Augsburg in Germany in the year of our Lord 1530 and the small Catechism of Luther.[18]

For Muus, Mohn, and their successors, St. Olaf was intended to be a place where the human spirit would be nurtured in conversation with the arts, the sciences, and the traditions of the Lutheran church. It was meant to be a place where Christ and culture could engage.[19]

### Christ and Culture Engaged

It was a risky gambit and not without its critics among church people. Georg Sverdrup was among the severest of St. Olaf's antagonists. He scored it as a bastion of "secularism" and "humanism" unfit for Christian youth.[20] And there were skeptics in the constituency of the United Church as well. Christians ought not, it was held, be exposed to Latin and Greek authors, studies in philosophy and literature, and all else that went with training in the liberal arts. This, it was held, would diffuse and undermine Christian certainty. Further the college ought, some said, to operate in close collaboration with the theological seminary rather than independently.

Mohn, in those early years, was the chief defender of the college's program. In response to the critics, he reiterated the commitment of the college to the suspect disciplines, precisely for the sake of the school's larger purposes. The critics were not, of course, instantly silenced. The college, however, survived and remained on its charted course. In doing so it exemplified the spirit of the United Norwegian Church, a spirit of mission and unity.

The mission of the college was from the first construed in terms of its immediate context. It aimed at the nurture of Christian individuals who would carry a closely cultivated sense of that primary vocation into other roles as citizens, workers, mothers, fathers, friends, and more. An apocryphal oral tradition records that President Lars W. Boe (1918-42) was once asked by a prominent churchman why St. Olaf bothered with educating women. Boe answered: "Because they become mothers." To contemporary ears the response is unhappily restrictive. Yet Boe had a point to make, and it is important that he made it with respect to women as well as men: the place for an education and the Christian faith to be put to work is the world as it is, the world of home and daily work. A Christian education was not, in the judgment of St. Olaf's founders, something to be saved for the theologians.

With a mission so defined, St. Olaf helped to make the United Church a denomination able to engage early and aggressively with the American context. It is not accidental that as the 19th century closed and the 20th opened leaders of the United Church were assessing realistically the church's ethnic character and beginning to see clearly the need for an English-speaking ministry, for an English-speaking church, and for a church beginning to think and act in an American manner—all for the sake of the church's mission.

### *Mission around the Globe*

Church and college fostered a sense of mission that extended beyond America to the globe. Large numbers of missionaries, like those of the family Søvik, went from the college through the church across the oceans. In 1911 the United Church established a chair of missions at its seminary and its first occupant was a graduate of St. Olaf College, M. J. Stolee. When the United

Church Seminary passed into the hands of the Norwegian Lutheran Church of America in 1917 and into those of The American Lutheran Church in 1960, the chair remained and it continued to be occupied by missionaries and theologians who had graduated from the school in Northfield: Rolf Syrdal, Andrew Burgess, and Paul Martinson.

The work of global mission is not, of course, without its risks. It means, among other things, the engagement of Christ with more than one culture. Missionaries often learn to see Christian and cultural things with new eyes and so foment growth and sometimes contention in the church. In the 1920s several Protestant denominations found themselves troubled by questions from the mission fields. It was a contentious time for American Christians as they struggled over Fundamentalism and Modernism and watched William Jennings Bryan and Clarence Darrow battle at the famed "monkey trial" in Dayton, Tennessee. Now quite at home in the United States, the Norwegian-American Lutherans were not immune to American controversies. When probing questions about Christ, cultures, and mission were raised among them, it was often by missionaries nurtured in the traditions of St. Olaf College and the United Church.[21]

### *Unity*

Missionaries, domestic and those at work around the globe, are often in the vanguard of those seeking greater Christian unity. It is not, therefore, surprising that the missionary traditions, domestic and foreign, of St. Olaf College and the United Church nurtured leaders in the search for unity among North American Lutherans.

The early association of the college with the Anti-Missourian cause meant that the school, the United Church, and the union movement among Norwegian-American Lutherans were born in the same cradle. An Anti-Missourian legacy marked church and college permanently.

The Madison Agreement ending the election controversy was strongly backed in the United Church and among the constituency of the college, where there was wide support for the second form. This settlement meant the end of an exhausting battle for the theologians, the beginnings of a theological reckoning with the American context, and the possibility of union among the Norwegian-American Lutherans. For better or for worse, the traditions of St. Olaf and the United Church had favored the introduction of the notion of options into theology and an end to the countervailing notion that church unity required complete agreement in doctrine and practice. The Madison Agreement had the further effect of permanently alienating the Norwegian-American Lutherans from the Missouri Synod and its synodical allies. The official resolution of the election controversy, strongly supported by the constituencies of St. Olaf and the United Church, thus set Norwegian-American Lutheranism on a course which eventually made The American Lutheran Church possible.

While by no means always playing principal roles, inheritors of the traditions of the United Church and St. Olaf College appear at nearly all the critical moments in which Norwegian-American Lutherans and their inheritors have had part in bringing U.S. Lutherans as a whole together. Four figures represent two chapters in the story.

Johan Arndt Aasgaard, a graduate of St. Olaf and ordained in the United Church, served as the second president of the Norwegian Lutheran Church of America. He helped to guide the church into the American Lutheran Conference, a cooperative federation of midwestern Lutherans. While Aasgaard's approach was cautious, he was persistently pestered and urged on to more decisive and vigorous action in the interests of Lutheran unity by his close friend and schoolmate at St. Olaf, Lars W. Boe, a pastor of the United Church before he became president of the college in 1918.

Fredrik A. Schiotz, Aasgaard's successor and another St. Olaf graduate, followed a cautious course similar to that of his predecessor, this time slowly and carefully guiding the church into the union forming The ALC of 1960. E. Clifford Nelson consistently urged Schiotz to even more inclusive action. Another alumnus of the college and an acute student of the Anti-Missourian movement and the traditions of the United Church, Nelson served the church as pastor, historian, professor and dean at Luther Theological Seminary, and finally as professor of religion at St. Olaf. Standing in the inheritance of the college and the United Church, and with sights adjusted to a new and broader context, Nelson steadily called on the church to avoid a preoccupation with the Missouri Synod and to move toward union with all ready to join in the cause of a confessional and evangelical Lutheranism.

### A Church and a College for the World

As a part of the discussion preliminary to the contemplated union of three Lutheran churches in this decade, representatives of 29 Lutheran colleges and universities met in 1983 with representatives of those laying plans for the new church. A report of that meeting said, ''There seemed to be general agreement that the place of a liberal arts Lutheran college ought to be somewhere between a Bible school and a totally secular university.''[22]

The vision of the founders of St. Olaf College was a clearer one. They proposed that their college be both a Bible school *and* a college ''plain and simple.'' It was a daring vision and a taxing one. How their inheritors have served the vision is a question for another place. The early history is, however, plain. Insofar as the builders of St. Olaf College succeeded in acting on their vision they helped make it possible for the United Norwegian Lutheran Church to be a church for the world. The legacy of that church endures to the present in The American Lutheran Church. It remains, for the future, open to critical appropriation.

Lutheran Free (1897)

# Free and Living Congregations
## How Can Congregational Freedom Be Assured?

by Gracia Grindal

One of the most persistent questions today in the Lutheran church is the question of freedom and authority.

We feel it most keenly when we think of how to structure a church body so that individual Christians may exercise as freely as possible their Christian vocations of service wherever they find themselves in life. Church structures should be created in order to enable, rather than hinder, the Christian's vocation. At the same time Lutherans, in particular, seek to ensure that the faith being proclaimed in the congregation is being accurately represented, for our tradition is a teaching tradition, one which cares about its theological legacy.

Georg Sverdrup, president and leader of Augsburg Seminary in Minneapolis for 33 years, thought long and hard about that question. Those of us thinking about a new Lutheran church in our country would do well to consider his theological work on this particular issue. An examination of his life and theology can be instructive to us in these days of church unification, even as it can teach us about one of the lesser known but distinctive traditions which make up The American Lutheran Church. Few people exemplify more clearly than Georg Sverdrup the peculiar and fiercely independent heritage which the Lutheran Free Church brought to The ALC when it united with it in 1963.

Sverdrup understood, as few before or since, that freedom comes from *unity*, not plurality. All his work toward the establishing of a theological school and a United Norwegian Lutheran Church in the last quarter of the 19th century—even his failure to compromise the future of Augsburg Seminary—comes from a Sverdrup understanding that is paradoxical. Sverdrup insisted that there could be no living and vital Christian freedom if the pastors of the church did not receive the same, common education (both in seminary and in preseminary schooling), one which was relevant to the needs of the emigrants, a free people in a free land.

### Congregation as Bedrock

Sverdrup knew that genuine freedom was vital to the life of any congregation and thus to the spiritual life of every Christian. But he also feared that a poorly educated laity—and clergy— might be tempted to make their personal experience and reading of the Bible the authority and norm for the Christian life. Free congregations were not complete without pastors who were to be the theological fulcrums of congregational life and mission. Parish members were each given a variety of gifts by God, but they were to be freely exercised by the members only if the gifts were mutually edifying. The work of the congregation—pastors and laity together—was to be constantly engaged in dialog as to what was edifying and good.

A personal Christianity without a rich congregational involvement was impossible to Sverdrup, who criticized the work of Kierkegaard and the more extreme of the individualistic pietists for their failure to include the congregation as the bedrock of all personal Christianity.

So it then followed that the pastors of these congregations needed a rigorous and careful education in biblical and historical

Georg Sverdrup
1848-1907

theology—the biblical languages and the Christian tradition—in order to interpret and teach the faith to the laity, even as they, the pastors, served them as Christ served the church. No biblical passage is so dear to Sverdrup on this issue as Ephesians 5, on the relation of Christ and the church.

At its loftiest, Sverdrup could be said to have understood Luther's notion of the priesthood of all believers in its most radical essence, sensing that it could finally be tried in America where no prince or parliament could interfere with the church's life, as had always been the trouble in Europe. But at its worst, Sverdrup could be said to have been a stubborn Norwegian who thought only his idea was right and who, upon not getting his own way, left the larger church body to itself so he could create Augsburg in his own image—smaller, perhaps, but purer than it might have been. As is generally the case, the truth lies somewhere in the middle of the two extreme interpretations.

### Aristocratic Origins

Georg Sverdrup was born December 16, 1848, in Balestrand, Norway, a small village at the end of the Sogne Fjord, one of the most beautiful and rugged regions of Norway. His father, Harald Ulrich Sverdrup, was a pastor who also served in the Storting, the national parliament. One of H. U. Sverdrup's major causes in parliament was the reform of the state church to a more congregational form of government. He is, however, most famous for his revision of Eric Pontoppidan's explanation to Luther's Small Catechism, English versions of which most Norwegian-Americans learned by heart when they "read for the minister" on their way to being confirmed.

Born into a family of the Dano-Norwegian aristocracy, Georg's character was shaped by the events and cultural situation in the Norway of his youth. Nationalism was flourishing as Norwegians sought to free themselves of Swedish political and cultural domination and to discover what was unique to the Norwegian character. The young Georg arrived in Christiania (now known as Oslo) in 1865 to study at the university. It was the year in which Ibsen completed his drama *Brand*. Two years later Ibsen would be finished with *Peer Gynt*, another play which explored the Norwegian character and soul. Without a doubt, Georg Sverdrup drank deeply of that literature and thought much about what it meant to be a Norwegian and a free person as he was growing up and studying, both under his father's tutelage in Sogn and at the university in Christiania. Though Norway was alive with many conflicts and debates over a number of nationalistic political issues during Sverdrup's student years, none was so significant to him as the debate over the place of the state in the work of the church.

Ever since the coming of Lutheranism to Norway—by princely decree—the church had been under the crown. Pastors were state officials responsible for a variety of government services in their geographically defined parishes, as well as preachers of the Word. This situation was a great offense to the pietists. Under the leadcrship of the great Norwegian lay preacher, Hans Nielsen Hauge (1771-1824), they sought to kindle in the hearts of the Norwegian folk a greater, more personal faith (see Chapter 3). A royal edict (*Konventikelplakat* 1741) frowned on any religious gathering in which a properly ordained pastor was not present. The state used this edict rather harshly against the pietists, especially Hauge, who spent some 10 years in jail for illegal religious activities. Though the law was abrogated in 1842, six years before Georg Sverdrup was born, the pietists—usually peasants or farmers living in the western parts of Norway—continued to feel strongly that the state church was filled with "dead orthodoxy." By its very structure, the pietists felt, this state church prevented the growth of either a warm personal faith or a free congregation in which such a living faith could be nurtured.

### Norway's Church-State Debate

By the 1850s the question of the relation between state and church was a serious national debate. Georg Sverdrup's uncle, Johan Sverdrup, also an elected member of the Storting and later to become prime minister of Norway (1884-89), cast his political lot with the landed farmers. They were something like a middle class, frequently pietists, and generally from Norway's western regions. With them Sverdrup formed Norway's first political party, the *Venstre* (the Left). The struggles of that party to separate the state from the affairs of the church—which to this day have proven unsuccessful—were the stuff of young Georg's life.

But it was not simply family loyalty that convinced Georg of the need for a free congregation in a free country: it was his strong conviction that it was biblical and necessary for the revival of the Norwegian church. N. N. Rønning, a Norwegian-American who has written a biographical sketch of Sverdrup, relates that Sverdrup once spoke of the difficulties of the congregations in such a system as the state church.

The ministers were appointed to serve parishes established along geographical lines; all persons inside the boundaries belonged to the church and were baptized and confirmed. It was a system where the minister was the only active person, the people were simply receiving what the minister gave them.[1]

Rønning says in that same article: "Other churchmen came from Norway to preach, to teach and to work along time-honored lines. Sverdrup came to blaze new trails."[2] The United States was a perfect laboratory for him in which to work out the ideas concerning the free congregation and spiritual life which he had developed during his early years in Norway.

He was ready, then, when he received the invitation to come to America to teach at the fledgling Augsburg Seminary in Minneapolis in 1874. Having graduated from the university in theology in 1871, he had spent a year in Paris studying Semitic languages and discussing plans for a free church with a compatriot of his, Sven Oftedal, who was to be his life-long colleague at Augsburg. Little is known of Sverdrup's activities between graduation and his coming to America, but it is fairly certain he traveled extensively throughout Europe, visiting in Erlangen and Rome, where the catacombs made a vivid impression on him.

August Weenaas, president and only teacher at Augsburg Seminary, had founded the school in Marshall (near Madison), Wisconsin, in 1869, after a separation from Augustana Seminary in Rock Island. Once Augsburg had moved to Minneapolis and it looked as though it would be a growing concern, Weenaas and the church body he represented, the Norwegian-Danish Conference, asked both Sverdrup and another Norwegian scholar, Sven Gunnersen, to come and teach in Minneapolis. The invitation was strongly encouraged by Sven Oftedal, who had come to join Weenaas at Augsburg the year before.

### New Church, New Land

Augsburg Seminary served the Norwegian-Danish Conference,

or simply the Conference, as it came to be known. It had been formed in 1870 by C. L. Clausen and others who had left the older Norwegian Synod (centered at Luther College, Decorah, Iowa) because of its refusal to condemn slavery as sin, and its more hierarchical structure (see Chapter 5). The call to teach at Augsburg represented for Sverdrup and Oftedal a chance to carry out their dreams for a church in which neither the exercise of personal piety nor the life of free congregations could be interfered with by either state or ecclesiastical structures from the past.

One hears this dream in Sverdrup's first address to the crowds who welcomed him to Augsburg in August of 1874, nine days after his arrival in Minneapolis. Reading it one sees the newcomer, a mere 26 years old, seizing the opportunity to speak of his dreams for a new church in a new land.

Georg and Mrs. Sverdrup (Catharine Heiberg), plus colleague Sven Gunnersen and his wife (Elizabeth Welhaven), are welcomed at Trinity congregation (the church known as the mother congregation of both Augsburg Seminary and the Lutheran Free Church). Sverdrup speaks prophetically of his reason for leaving Norway and accepting the call of the Conference to teach at its seminary. Commenting on the troubled situation in the Norwegian-American church, he notes that

> . . . few had come over [from Norway] who were able to become guides and teachers, pastors and shepherds for those who after all were baptized unto Christ and confessed our Lutheran faith. And in our eyes the distress was increased by the fact that strife and disruptions were rampant among the congregations which had been organized here. But we saw also that this church group [the Conference] in whose midst we stand tonight, had with clear vision seen the true remedy against the distress. For by founding its theological school it had expressed the great and logical principle that *the Norwegian people in America also in this respect must become able to take care of themselves.*[3]

Very likely as a student at Christiania University he had watched with dismay the arguments concerning abolition and slavery, which were vigorously debated not only in the Norwegian-American press but also in the church press of Norway. His sense that the Norwegian Synod was too much under the influence of the German-origin Missouri Synod must have been formed rather clearly when in 1867 Herman Amberg Preus, president of the Norwegian Synod, gave seven lectures at Christiania on the religious situation among the emigrants in America.[4] The lectures are careful descriptions of the state of the Norwegian-American Lutheran churches. But Preus, unfortunately for himself and his Synod, chose to defend the rather unpopular theological opinion that slavery was not a *sin*, but rather a *moral evil*, an opinion which cut about as much mustard with the people in Norway as it did in the North of the U.S. It caused an uproar in both the religious and secular press in Norway, one from which the Norwegian Synod in the U.S. could not easily extricate itself.

Sverdrup, as a young idealistic democrat, reacted against such theological hairsplitting, as he also did against the increasingly individualistic Christianity promulgated at the time by the more extreme of the Norwegian-American pietists. In many ways, he was ideally situated to become a leader of the middle way in Norwegian-American Lutheranism. That is where he belonged. But, ultimately, it was not to be so.

### Germans in Missouri

As a student his opinions on these issues could be more virulent than they might have been in actual church work. It is important to remember that he was able to benefit, at long distance, from the work of the Norwegian Synod, seasoned by more than two decades of experiences which he could only imagine in Norway. One might almost argue that it was the efforts of those who founded Luther College, as a first step toward actually building a seminary or *presteskole*, which gave Sverdrup the luxury of being able to step off the train in Minneapolis and launch into a speech which sharply criticized the Synod and its failure to build its own seminary. (Instead, the Synod for 23 years sent its ministerial candidates to study with the German Missourians in St. Louis.) Sverdrup foresaw a unique kind of seminary education that would produce pastors fit for the Norwegian-American church. One can hear that in his concluding remarks at Trinity Church that August day in 1874.

> We stand here filled with the conviction that we are in more than one sense in the land of the future, because this is the land of freedom. We are convinced that the Norwegian people here have a great and glorious calling, this namely, to declare the truth that freedom is not without God, but in God; to bear witness that freedom and Christianity are not two things, but one. In order that the Norwegian people shall make this calling a reality wherever it is found in the world, abroad and at home, for this we work, for this we live.[5]

One can see that Sverdrup's concern for political freedom, and the freedom of the congregation as the fundamental unit of the Christian church—plus its place as the nourisher of personal religious life—are all to be found in their essence here. One also can read in this piece the pure eloquence of his speech, an eloquence which translates well because of its balanced style. Rønning remarked that "the first time I heard him lecture I was struck by the clarity and logical presentation of thought. He spoke with authority. . . . Wherever you find a Sverdrup, there is a man who thinks straight and makes the words go home."[6] Georg Sverdrup was the kind of speaker whose eloquence and character could move people to follow him and remain loyal. It was a skill he used to great effect throughout his life.

### Renewal in Norway as Well?

The rest of Sverdrup's days would be spent working out his idea of freedom and its implications for the American situation.

And yet, one can sense in almost all his work the hope that the Norwegian-Americans, by establishing a congregational form of the church, would bring renewal not only to the church in America (already, by his lights, corrupted by state-church tendencies within the Norwegian Synod), but also to the church in Norway.

Understanding the passion of Sverdrup to reform the church at home, as well as in the U.S., we can then begin to understand much of the rest of his work in the establishment of both Augsburg Seminary and the Lutheran Free Church.

The words "free congregation" and "personal Christianity" run through the rest of his work like the proverbial red thread. He and his colleagues began to design and develop an educational institution which would train pastors for work in the new congregations being established in the ever-westward movement of the Norwegian emigrants in their search for cheap and fertile land. Sverdrup wanted a clergy trained to be open to the new opportunities and situation of the frontiers, ministers who would not stand on inherited or supposed privileges, who would be servants of the congregation rather than ecclesiastical tyrants.

It was Sverdrup's opinion (and that of most Norwegian-American church leaders) that pastors trained in Norway were woefully unprepared for the frontier church. Either they simply failed in their ministry and had to return home or they had to be carefully retrained for the new work. Sverdrup regretted the many different kinds of education the pastors of the Norwegian-American churches had received and supposed that peace would replace the strife among them only when all the pastors had received the same education *and* when there had been a revival and awakening in the congregations, similar to those of the Hauge revivals in Norway. From 1874 until 1893 Sverdrup was able to pilot Augsburg Seminary along this line of thought.

His dream of making Augsburg the theological training center for most Norwegian-American pastors almost came to be in the 1890s. The story of the failure of Sverdrup to get his plan accepted by the Norwegian Lutheran churches in America is a tale of bitterness and missed opportunities, all of which have been told in other places.[7] In the main it involved a controversy over the place of two schools, St. Olaf and Augsburg, in the new United Norwegian Lutheran Church which Sverdrup was instrumental in designing. Sverdrup and those in the Augsburg party did not want to lose their dream of a single school—where seminary and "university" could be together—in which future pastors were carefully trained from high school through seminary. Their feeling that they had developed an innovative curriculum that produced pastors ready and able to meet the peculiar challenges of the American church was too strong to allow them to give up their preparatory department (later to become Augsburg College) in favor of St. Olaf.

When it appeared that they would not get their way, the Augsburg party removed themselves from the United Church and a group known as the Friends of Augsburg became the sole supporters of Augsburg. For four years (1893 to 1897) they operated as a loose association which became the Lutheran Free Church in 1897.

### Planner of Union

As one who was raised in those wounds, I would prefer to examine Sverdrup at what I consider to be his most influential moment in the life of the church: his leadership during the union discussions which led to the formation of the United Church in 1890.

Disunity had been a fact of Norwegian-American church life ever since the first three Norwegian pastors (each of differing opinion on church doctrine and polity) arrived in this country to care for their flocks. All during Sverdrup's tenure at Augsburg there were calls for church unity and several free conferences of interested church people were held during the 1880s to discuss and debate certain theses which might become the basis for church union. But by the end of the 1880s, after a schism in the Norwegian Synod caused by a predestination controversy, a group calling itself the Anti-Missourian Brotherhood, centered in the St. Olaf College community, invited the other Norwegian churches into specific merger talks. Not wanting either to become a separate church body or to join forces with an already existing group, the Anti-Missourians proposed that they, the Hauge Synod, the Conference, and the Norwegian Augustana Synod begin serious talks toward a new church.

Despite suspicions about the intentions of the Anti-Missourian Brotherhood (led by one of the first teachers at Luther College, F. A. Schmidt), Sverdrup had long been urging the union of the various synods of the Norwegian-American Lutherans. Sent by the Conference as its delegate to a planning meeting in Eau Claire, Wisconsin, August 15-28, 1888, Sverdrup soon became the leading force on the subcommittee charged with writing the articles of union. And when the report from the subcommittee on doctrine did not meet with the approval of the larger committee, Sverdrup and the other three theological professors at the meeting wrote one that did.

Sverdrup persuaded the committee of theologians that it should concentrate on the ideas and beliefs the various communions held in common. The groups found they could unanimously accept the Holy Scriptures, the confessions of the Norwegian church, and the Small Catechism of Martin Luther with its explanation by Bishop Erik Pontoppidan (*Truth unto Godliness*) as the basis for their union. Following that statement of essential unity was a statement noting that the disagreements which still existed were not sufficiently serious to keep the groups apart; it concluded with a mutual confession of faults. Then the statement examined the problems surrounding the individual points of difference, arguments Lutherans have been having ever since the beginning: atonement and justification, the gospel, and absolution.

The question of lay activity was also a burning one for these people who had been so deeply affected by Hans Nielsen Hauge. This was a matter close to Sverdrup's heart. He thought the idea that the laity could preach only in an emergency (*nødprincip*), a principle developed by Gisle Johnson, his professor at Christiania, too negative a way of putting the statement. In Sverdrup's rewriting it is put more positively:

> We declare our conviction that it [lay activity] has been a source of great blessing in our Church and among our people, and we believe that it ought earnestly to be recommended and promoted among us. This activity in its true form we do not consider to be any intrusion into the office of the ministry, and therefore it is not in conflict with Article XIV of the Augsburg Confession.[8]

Though this was a strong statement for the work of the laity, the Hauge Synod members did not think it strong enough and eventually withdrew from the merger proceedings.

### Sverdrup Retained Lay Identity

It is of interest to note here that Sverdrup was not ordained and frequently identified with his hearers as "we laymen." Why he chose to remain unordained is not a matter of public record, other than that the practical course (leading to pastoral service) at the University of Christiania seemed to him to be uniformly dreary. It could be that he did not feel himself called to be a pastor—only a teacher of pastors—and took seriously the call of the congregation, believing it was not for him. Or it could be that, with one of his successors as Augsburg president, Bernhard Christensen, he felt that the New Testament did not require any further ordination for ministry than Baptism. In any case, it is a tantalizing fact that needs further discussion and might help us today as we try to figure out just what the ordained ministry is.

When the committees submitted the Articles of Union and a proposed constitution, it was generally agreed that Sverdrup's work had been fundamental to the success of the groups. His hand is most obvious in the proposed name of the organization: The Norwegian Lutheran Free Church in America. What followed in the constitution focused on making the congregations the center of the work of the church, with little power seated in the church body. The church convention had some powers: to advise the congregations and to make decisions regarding the educational mission of the church. The church was to meet in convention yearly and was to be made up of one lay delegate from each congregation and its pastor, plus the theological professors of the seminary.

When these articles were presented to the committee, the name was changed to the United Norwegian Lutheran Church in America, a clear defeat for Sverdrup. But a greater defeat loomed in the future when Sverdrup's dream for Augsburg as the school for pastors in the new church did not materialize.

But for the moment there was great joy among the three synods forming the United Norwegian Lutheran Church. After years of splintering, many of the Norwegian Lutherans in America were returning to each other. When the new body met in convention on June 13, 1890, a dramatic celebration began. The Anti-Missourians, who were gathered in St. Paul's Church, a well-known Hauge Synod church in Minneapolis, and the Norwegian Augustana Synod representatives, who were assembled at Augsburg Seminary, marched to Trinity Church, where the members of the Conference awaited them. When all three groups were together, a short service of thanksgiving was held; then the entire group moved to the Swedish Augustana Synod church nearby, which was large enough to accommodate the mass gathering. Sven Oftedal was elected temporary chairman of the first annual meeting of the United Church and the constitution, largely a product of Sverdrup's work, was ratified immediately.

### Disillusionment Comes Early

Though in many ways a triumph for Sverdrup, that convention was also the beginning of his increasing disillusionment with how things were working out. The struggle focused on control of two institutions named Augsburg: the seminary and the publishing house, which the United Church was to establish in 1891.

The story of the battle over the two Augsburgs is incredibly complicated. At issue was who owned Augsburg Seminary. During the negotiations leading to the merger of 1890, it was hoped by many that the United Church would make Augsburg the seminary of the new church. A plan was developed to transfer Augsburg Seminary's property to the United Church. But the Augsburg party feared they would lose control of their preparatory school in favor of St. Olaf College in Northfield, also supported by people of the United Church.

Sverdrup and Oftedal feared, with some reason, that the St. Olaf supporters would not keep their promises to Augsburg after the Augsburg party relinquished its control to the larger body, the United Church. Even though there was fairly good evidence that the church as a whole favored making Augsburg the college as well as the seminary of the new church, ill will against the failure of the Augsburg party to compromise was growing.

By the 1893 convention of the United Church feelings were running high. Sverdrup and Oftedal resigned as professors of the United Church, but not of Augsburg Seminary. Delegates friendly to Sverdrup and Oftedal met and, in time, became a group known as "The Friends of Augsburg." They would become, in 1897, the Lutheran Free Church.

Following the 1893 convention, when Augsburg Seminary seemed to be neither in nor out of the United Church, Augsburg Publishing House, housed in North Hall on the Augsburg campus, became the center of the controversy. Who owned the books and

Original building of Augsburg Publishing House at Augsburg College

who had control of the two church papers and the printing equipment was not clear.

The publishing house was directed by the board of trustees of Augsburg Seminary. The manager of the publishing house was Lars Swenson, who was also treasurer of the seminary and of the United Church. The Augsburg board did not trust him. On June 15, 1893, they fired him and appointed Halvor Engemoen in his place. Two days later, while Swenson was away on business, Oftedal and Engemoen entered the publishing house building, told the employees to leave, and changed the locks on the door.

The confrontation was tense and ugly. It was not solved until a year later, after litigation which awarded the publishing house to the United Church. By then, the schism between the Augsburg party and the majority party in the United Church was nearly complete. In 1895 the convention of the United Church refused to seat Sverdrup and Oftedal as delegates from Trinity congregation. That action was the darkest moment of the controversy and mortally wounded any chance for reconciliation until 1963, when most of the LFC did at last join the other Norwegian-Americans in The ALC.

## *"Fundamental Principles"*

When the Friends of Augsburg became the Lutheran Free Church in 1897, its founding principles contained Sverdrup's purest thought concerning the congregation. As Eugene Fevold remarks, "no document associated with the history of the Lutheran Free Church is more important than the 'Fundamental Principles' adopted at its second annual meeting in 1898."[9] Foremost of the principles is the first, one which was burned into the mind of every thoughtful member of the LFC, even up to its entry into The ALC in 1963: "According to the Word of God, the congregation is the right form of the Kingdom of God on earth."

It is difficult to explain to those on the outside how passionately that principle was held by members of the LFC. The rugged individualists who had broken the prairies of northern and western Minnesota and North Dakota, or who went further west into Washington state, the regions where Sverdrup's message was most warmly received, responded to him and his ideas with loyalty and reverence. His picture was almost as prominent in those homes as was that of Abraham Lincoln, another hero of freedom to the Norwegian immigrants. Many attics throughout those areas may still have dusty framed pictures of the handsome Sverdrup.

He was a man of conviction and wry humor. The story is told that once a young man came to him and said that it was God's will that he be allowed to get on with his ministry and not study any more Greek, Hebrew, or Latin. Sverdrup is reported to have replied, "Well, that's all well and good, but I'm in charge here."

Most remembrances of him are of a man of quiet reserve who loved theological debate. He is reported to have said in his later life that he most loved walking against a fierce winter storm.[10]

That same zest could be seen in his appetite for theological controversy.

His greatest legacy to the church today is his theological writings and the institutions he helped to found. Those who are able to read his work in Norwegian can only be amazed at how much there is. Andreas Helland gathered some representative writings from his work in the various journals of the Norwegian-American church press and produced six volumes!''

Sverdrup not only edited the major organ of the Conference, *Lutheraneren* (The Lutherans), 1877-81 and 1885-90, he was also a frequent contributor to, and for two years coeditor of, the independent weekly paper of Sven Oftedal, *Folkebladet* (People's Paper). From 1875 to 1881 he edited *Kvartalskrift* (The Quarterly), the theological journal of the Conference. And from 1890 to 1893 he edited the United Church's periodical, *Kirkebladet* (Church Paper). Further, he started a journal in 1900 to support the mission in Madagascar, *Gasseren* (The Malagasy), editing it until his death in 1907.

Add the heavy load he had in teaching both Old Testament and systematic theology at the seminary, plus his duties as president of the school. Nor should one fail to mention his role in the founding of the Lutheran Deaconess Home. If one adds to all this his countless speaking engagements throughout the Midwest, one might be able to gain a small sense of the force this man had on his time and people.

Through all of it there is the theme of freedom and the free congregation. All his work and thought flows from that fundamental set of principles. But one would be wrong to suggest that Sverdrup's passionate concern for the free congregation was an end in itself. He saw it as the best way to organize the Kingdom of God on earth.

His enthusiasm for foreign mission resulted in the sending out of the first missionaries from the Norwegian-American churches,

Elizabeth Fedde
1850-1923
founder of
Deaconess Hospital,
Minneapolis

two Augsburg graduates, Pastors John Hogstad and Erik H. Tou.[12] Sverdrup based his support for the deaconess movement, which founded Lutheran Deaconess Hospital in Minneapolis, on the need congregations would have for sending deaconesses out into the communities around them. He argued that women who had not been called to be wives and mothers needed other avenues for serving God. The fact that the Friends of Augsburg, and later LFC annual meetings, let women be voting delegates brought him and the organization nothing but scorn and contempt. But it is a testimony to the integrity of his theological and democratic principles that he valued the work of women as members of the laity whose gifts were gifts to the church, with as much significance as the gifts of either the clergy or the laymen.

### *Out of the Mainstream*

So it is possible to regret that Georg Sverdrup lost his chance to become the driving theological force in the new United Church.

As Warren Quanbeck notes in his introduction to Melvin Helland's translation of some Sverdrup writings,

> It is one of the tragic developments in the history of Norwegian Lutheranism that Georg Sverdrup, one of her best prepared and most prophetic theologians, should have moved away from the mainstream and have been thrust into a minority situation. The formation of the United Norwegian Lutheran Church in 1890 seemed to promise much through concentration of strong leadership and vigorous congregations. But tensions and suspicions soon arose, especially over the question of theological education. . . . Sverdrup, who had thought of his work as being the nurturing of a movement within Norwegian Lutheranism, now found himself leader of a small segment of it. The responsibilities and burdens of leadership and administration took their toll of his theological productivity. Even more damaging to Norwegian-American Lutheranism was Sverdrup's isolation from the more numerous church groups. His influence might have helped prevent the excursion into scholastic and even fundamentalistic theology which blighted much Lutheran preaching and pastoral practice in the next generations. . . . Sverdrup's insight and eloquence could have strengthened the cause of a historically informed theology, a healthier evangelism and a more ecumenical and open churchmanship.[13]

It is instructive to read the later history of the LFC to see how Sverdrup's ideals did or did not drive that group. One of the more revealing moments in the history of the LFC is when it finally had to admit that, instead of being a movement in the Norwegian-American church, it was really a church body, something that did not happen until 1927 when it officially approved a model constitution for congregations. In it was the provision that the congregation "subscribed to the LFC's 'Fundamental Principles and Rules for Work' (Article III)."[14] Until that time, and even after, it was difficult to tell exactly which congregations were part of the LFC. Apparently many congregations within the LFC felt that even such a minor thing as the national group asking congregations to subscribe officially to its Fundamental Principles was going beyond the bounds of Sverdrup's Principles. And it was not until 1959 that the LFC annual meeting was able to adopt a delegate system of congregation representation to the annual meeting. Before that, anyone declaring him or herself to be in sympathy with the Principles of the LFC was free to vote at the annual meeting.

Sverdrup's spirit lived on in the Lutheran Free Church most clearly in its ecumenical developments through the years. Finding good reasons for cooperating with other Lutherans, the LFC was able to participate in the National Lutheran Council, the American Lutheran Conference, and many other joint Lutheran projects. Where it always drew the line was on any threat to its congregational polity, which it made a matter of dogma rather than mere order. It was for reasons of church polity that it voted repeatedly not to consider organic church union until, finally, in 1963 it had amended its Rules enough to allow the consistent majority of its congregations, which had regularly voted for merger, to have its way. (Even then, some 40 of 330 LFC congregations chose to stay outside the ALC; most of them joined the Association of Free Lutheran Churches.)

### Early Death

The cost of losing Sverdrup's vision for the larger Norwegian-American church can only be imagined today, though now, perhaps, we can return to those old conflicts with less passion and bad blood. But the loss the Lutheran Free Church itself felt when Sverdrup died an untimely death in his 59th year, May 3, 1907, is an indication of the importance of the man and his theology for his people.

The shock that went through the Augsburg community and the LFC when they heard of their leader's death has been told by

poets,[15] biographers, and casual observers. The notes for his intended graduation address at Augsburg the day of his death indicate that he was going to speak on "the free people and the
free man" and "the value of truth."

After Sverdrup's body was taken from Augsburg where it had
lain in state all morning, to Trinity Church, where mourners filled
the sanctuary to capacity and hundreds more stood outside in the
dismal, grey chill of the rainy afternoon, the funeral service began. Sven Oftedal, Sverdrup's long-time associate, preached the
sermon. At the end of the service, Oftedal presented a wreath on
behalf of the faculty of Augsburg Seminary and said, "Farewell,
friend! You were spirit of my spirit, thought of my thought, half
of my life." Some 60 or 70 carriages followed the casket to its
final resting place at Lakewood Cemetery in Minneapolis.

We at this distance have the advantage of history and can note
with reverence the remarkable and consistent integrity of Sverdrup's work on this earth. He had begun his days in America at
Trinity Church 33 years before, where he had spoken eloquently
of his mission in America: to work to establish a school where
truth and freedom were one, a school where pastors could learn
to serve free and living congregations.

In these days of anarchy and fear of authority, Sverdrup's passionate ideals can still be instructive to those of us looking for a
better way to nurture the life of the Spirit throughout the whole
church on earth.

# NOTES

## Introduction

1. E. Clifford Nelson and Eugene Fevold, *The Lutheran Church among Norwegian-Americans*, 2 vols. (Minneapolis: Augsburg, 1960), 1:90.
2. J. A. Bergh, *Den Norsk Lutherske Kirkes Historie i Amerika* (Minneapolis: Augsburg, 1914), p. 145.

## Chapter 1

1. All Stauch quotations are from his autobiography, written in German in 1843, and translated into English by his son Samuel in 1878. The original is in the Lutheran Seminary Library, Gettysburg, Pa.
2. A reference to the Old Testament figure, a priest who appears without ancestry or origin, with whom Christ is identified by the writer of Hebrews. See Gen. 14:18; Ps. 110:4; Hebrews 5 and 7.
3. This body, also known as the Ministerium of Pennsylvania, was organized in 1748 as the first formal fellowship of Lutheran congregations in North America. Other bodies organized prior to the Ohio Synod founding were the Synod of New York (1786) and the Synod of North Carolina (1803).
4. Ellis Beaver Burgess, *Memorial History of the Pittsburgh Synod of the Evangelical Lutheran Church, 1748-1845-1924* (Greenville, Pa.: Beaver Printing Co., 1925), p. 23.
5. A moving depiction of the land of Ohio as it greeted the first settlers is Conrad Richter's novel *The Trees* (New York: Alfred A. Knopf, 1940). This paragraph is a sample: ''Now they had crossed the Ohio

on a pole ferry. . . . For a moment Sayward reckoned that her father had fetched them unbeknownst to the Western ocean and what lay beneath was the late sun glittering on green-black water. Then she saw that what they looked down on was a dark, illimitable expanse of wilderness. It was a sea of solid treetops broken only by some gash where deep beneath the foliage an unknown stream made its way. As far as the eye could reach this lonely forest sea rolled on and on till its faint blue billows broke against an incredibly distant horizon'' (*The Trees*, p. 5).

6. Fred W. Meuser, *The Formation of the American Lutheran Church* (Columbus: Wartburg Press, 1958), pp. 7-9.

7. P. H. Buehring, *The Spirit of the American Lutheran Church* (Columbus: Lutheran Book Concern, 1940), p. 63.

8. Stauch was involved with theological education in Ohio before there were institutions for that purpose. As did many early pastors in the East, he trained a number of young men for the ministry by having them "read theology" with him. It meant they lived in his home, studied works in his meager library, accompanied him on some of his circuits—all the time letting them learn theology and ministry in constant interplay with each other. At least half a dozen of the early Ohio pastors were trained in this way.

9. The year of Stauch's death was a significant year for the other three German groups which would find themselves uniting in 1930 with the Joint Synod: in 1845 the Buffalo Synod was founded, immigrants who were to become part of the Synod in Texas were founding the community of New Braunfels, and forerunners of the Iowa Synod founders opened their first colony to evangelize Indians at Frankenmuth, Michigan.

10. When the American Lutheran Church was formed in 1930, Ohio Synod provided 56% of its membership, Iowa 35%, Texas 7%, and Buffalo 2%.

11. By Larry Hoffsis, ALC pastor in Dayton, Ohio, and chairman of the board of Trinity Lutheran Seminary, Columbus. Pastor Hoffsis is a son of the Sulphur Springs congregation which has custody of the cemetery.

## Chapter 2

1. Information for Grabau's early years through his emigration is drawn chiefly from the biography by his son, Johann A. Grabau: *Lebenslauf des ehrwuerdigen J. An. A. Grabau* (Buffalo: Reinecke und Zesch, 1879); quotations in this chapter not otherwise credited are from this book.

2. Fred W. Meuser, *The Formation of the American Lutheran Church* (Columbus: Wartburg Press, 1958), p. 14.

3. The Grabaus had four children, three of whom were born following emigration. One son, Johann A., also a Lutheran pastor, had seven children; three of them—John N., Rudolph, and Edward—became Lutheran pastors as well. A fourth son of Johann, Theodore, was a Lutheran parochial school teacher. His son, Harold T. (born 1909), is a member of the ALC clergy living in retirement in Texas.

4. Ernst N. Denef documents Buffalo's moderation in his "History of the Buffalo Synod," published in installments in *Wachende Kirche*, 1919-29. This German-language paper, founded by Grabau in 1866 and edited by him until his death in 1879, was published until the ALC merger in 1930.

5. Because of its small size, Buffalo did not establish many institutions. It maintained its Martin Luther Seminary until the ALC merger in 1930 and had organized a home mission society. Its international mission activity was carried out through fervent support of the Lutheran Orient Mission among the Kurds in what is now Iran.

6. Paul H. Buehring, *The Spirit of the American Lutheran Church* (Columbus: Wartburg Press, 1940), p. 24.

## Chapter 3

1. Einar Molland in *The Encyclopedia of the Lutheran Church*, 3 vols. (Minneapolis: Augsburg, 1965), 2:988.

2. M. O. Wee, *Haugeanism* (private publication: St. Paul, 1919), p. 620.

3. Sverre Norborg, *Hans Nielsen Hauge—Biografi 1804-1824* (Oslo: J. W. Cappelens Forlag, 1970), p. 189.

4. Jacob B. Bull, *Hans Nielsen Hauge* (Christiania: Steen'ske Boktrykkeri, 1909), p. 161.

5. Bull, p. 365.

6. *Ibid.*

7. Wee, pp. 56-57.

8. Andreas Aarflot, *Hans Nielsen Hauge—His Life and Message* (Minneapolis: Augsburg, 1979), p. 83.

9. Aarflot, p. 108.

10. *Samling af Religiøsebreve Skrevne af Hans Nielsen Hauge, Samt Hans Testament til Sine Venner* (Stavanger: Dreyers, 1872), pp. 146-147.

11. M. O. Wee, in *Mindebok for Hans Nielsen Hauge* (ed. M. O. Wee and O. E. Rolvaag; Minneapolis: Augsburg, 1926), p. 102.

12. Chr. O. Brohaugh and J. Eistensen, *Elling Eielsen Liv og Virksomhet* (Chicago: Skandinaven, 1883), p. 72.

13. J. Magnus Rohne, *Norwegian American Lutheranism up to 1872* (New York: Macmillan, 1926), p. 171.

14. J. C. K. Preus, *Norsemen Found a Church* (Minneapolis: Augsburg, 1953), p. 9.

15. J. A. Bergh, *Den Norsk Lutherske Kirkes Historie in Amerika* (Minneapolis: Augsburg, 1914), p. 41.

16. Rohne, p. 107.

17. Caroll Satre, in *Striving for Ministry* (ed. Warren A. Quanbeck; Minneapolis: Augsburg, 1977), p. 88.

18. E. Clifford Nelson and Eugene Fevold, *The Lutheran Church among Norwegian-Americans*, 2 vols. (Minneapolis: Augsburg, 1960), 1:148.

19. O. M. Norlie, *Den Forenede Norsk Lutherske Kirke i America* (Minneapolis: Augsburg, 1914), p. 5.

20. Arthur Rohl, ed., *Red Wing Seminary—Fifty Years of Service* (Red Wing, Minn.: n.p., 1930), p. 82.

21. *Budbaereren* [periodical of the Hauge Synod], 19, no. 45 (1887), p. 712.

22. *Budbaereren,* 21, no. 42 (1889), p. 638.

23. R. A. Syrdal, *White unto Harvest* (Minneapolis: Augsburg, 1934), p. 10.

24. *Budbaereren,* 23, no. 46 (1891), p. 30.

## Chapter 4

1. H. C. Ziehe, *A Centennial Story of the Lutheran Church in Texas 1851-1951*, 2 vols. (Seguin, Tex.: South Texas Printing Co., 1951-1954), 1:13-16.
2. Johannes Mgebroff, *Geschichte der ersten Deutschen Evangelische-Lutherischen Synode in Texas* (Chicago: Wartburg Publishing House, 1902), p. 11.
3. Erich Schick and Klaus Haag, *Christian Friedrich Spittler, Handlager Gottes* (Giessen: Brunnen-Verlag, 1982), p. 26.
4. Ibid., p. 43.
5. Ziehe, pp. 35-36. Two great-grandsons of C. A. Sager are pastors of The American Lutheran Church: Wilfred of Arlington, Texas, and Allan of Columbus, Ohio. There is no record that the Synod in Texas attempted any evangelism efforts among Indians.
6. Ziehe, p. 22.
7. Ziehe, p. 100. The departures were becoming so serious that at the Synod's 1854 convention the so-called "Texas Oath" was adopted by the pastors: "Resolved: none of us shall leave Texas unless his condition of health cannot stand up under the climate." Ziehe observes that "even some of those present at the convention later forgot; others evidently never placed themselves under the obligation."
8. Ziehe, p. 75.
9. Fred W. Meuser, *The Formation of the American Lutheran Church* (Columbus: Wartburg Press, 1958), p. 20.

## Chapter 5

1. E. Clifford Nelson and Eugene L. Fevold, *The Lutheran Church among Norwegian-Americans*, 2 vols. (Minneapolis: Augsburg, 1960).
2. Complete studies of the slavery debate appear in Theodore C. Blegen's *Norwegian Migration to America* (Northfield, Minn.: Norwegian-American Historical Association, 1931 and 1940), 2: 418-453; and J. Magnus Rohne's *Norwegian American Lutheranism up to 1872* (New York: The Macmillan Co., 1926), pp. 200-222. A helpful summary appears in Nelson and Fevold, pp. 169-180.

3. At the formation of the Norwegian Lutheran Church of America (1917) the Norwegian Synod contributed approximately 34% of the new church's membership, Hauge's Synod 9%, and the United Norwegian Church 57%. The Lutheran Free Church, also Norwegian, had 30,000 members but did not join in the merger.

4. For a sharp attack on the classical humanistic curriculum, see Georg Sverdrup's "Malaise of Humanism." Originally published in 1891, it was translated by Melvin Helland and published along with other Sverdrup selections in *The Heritage of Faith* (Minneapolis: Augsburg Publishing House, 1969). U. V. Koren, leader of the Norwegian Synod, responded with "Professor Sverdrup og Humanismens Princep," *Samlede Skrifter* (Decorah: Lutheran Publishing House, 1892), 3:112-125.

5. The Synod did not establish its own seminary until 1876, when a school was opened at Madison, Wisconsin. In 1855 the Synod sent a team to look into the possibility of affiliating with Buffalo's Martin Luther Seminary in Buffalo, Ohio's Capital Seminary in Columbus, or Missouri's Concordia Seminary in St. Louis. Concordia was chosen and soon Norwegian students were studying theology with Germans in St. Louis. A Norwegian professorship was opened in 1859 when Pastor Laur. Larsen, later to become the first president of Luther College, began teaching at Concordia. The arrangement was continued for nearly two decades.

6. Monika Hellwig, "Hope and Liberation: the Task of Sexual Complementarity," in *Readings in Christian Humanism* (ed. J. M. Shaw et al.; Minneapolis: Augsburg Publishing House, 1982), pp. 647-652.

7. Gracia Grindal, "The Sketchbook of Linka Preus" (unpublished). The sketches are in the archives of the Preus Library at Luther College, Decorah, Iowa.

## *Chapter 6*

1. Carl Krebs, "Selbstbiographie des Indianermissionars Carl Krebs," unpublished manuscript (Abschrift im Archiv des Missionswerks Neuendettelsau, West Germany, Nr. 41-42 "Krebs"), unpublished trans. by G. M. Schmutterer.

2. Albert Keiser, *Lutheran Mission Work among the American Indians* (Minneapolis: Augsburg Publishing House, 1922), p. 59. Chapter 3 contains an interesting description of the work by Lutherans among Chippewas in Michigan, 1842-69.

3. Quoted in G. J. Zeilinger, *A Missionary Synod with a Mission* (Chicago: Wartburg Publishing House, 1929), p. 19.

4. Edgar I. Steward, *Custer's Luck* (Norman: University of Oklahoma Press, 1955), p. 17.

5. John E. Sunder, *The Fur Trade on the Upper Missouri, 1840-1865* (Norman: University of Oklahoma Press, 1965), p. 143.

6. Dee Brown, *Bury My Heart at Wounded Knee* (New York: Bantam Books, 1970), p. 68.

7. Jakob Schmidt, "Aus dem Tagebuch des Missionars Schmidt in Nordamerika," *Missionsblatt* (March–November 1859); unpublished trans. by G. M. Schmutterer. The story of the 1858 journey is detailed in Schmidt's diary; the same trip is briefly described also in Sunder's *The Fur Trade on the Upper Missouri, 1840-1865* (see n. 5).

8. Zeilinger, p. 32.

9. Neither returned. Doederlein soon thereafter joined the Missouri Synod. Schmidt married Margarethe Lutz (a great-great-aunt of author Lutz) and accepted a call to an Iowa Synod congregation in Detroit. He died there in 1912.

10. Erwin Fritschel, "A History of the Indian Mission of the Lutheran Iowa Synod, 1856 to 1866" (unpublished dissertation, Colorado State College of Education, 1939), p. 49.

11. The seminary building at St. Sebald is long gone; its preparatory department was relocated to Galena, Illinois, in 1868, and the theological school moved to Mendota, Illinois, in 1874. But the cemetery and historic church, still serving a congregation of farm people, remain. To visit, drive west of Strawberry Point 1½ miles on Hwy. 3, then north 4 miles.

12. Zeilinger, p. 38.

## Chapter 7

1. R. Andersen, "Den Første Danske Jul i Amerika" [The First Danish Christmas in America], *Julegranen*, 1907 (Cedar Falls, Ia.: Holst Publishing Company, 1917).

2. A plaque in the Anglican Church of Churchill, Manitoba, reads: "In memory of Captain Jens Munk's expedition to Nova Dania, Hudson Bay, 1619-20, and Chaplain Rasmus Jensen, Aarhus . . . [who preached] his last sermon from his bed on January 23, 1620."

3. John O. Evjen, *Scandinavians in New York between 1630 and 1674* (Minneapolis: K. C. Holter, 1916). The Bronck family held farmland in what is today's borough of the Bronx, and New Amsterdamers early came to refer to the area as "the Broncks'."

4. John M. Jensen, *The United Evangelical Lutheran Church: An Interpretation* (Minneapolis: Augsburg, 1964), pp. 60-61.

5. The Danish Evangelical Lutheran Church changed its name in 1955 to American Evangelical Lutheran Church. Its national office was in Des Moines, where it opened Grand View College and Seminary in 1896. The college continues as a four-year institution; the seminary became part of the Lutheran School of Theology in Chicago in the 1960s.

6. Jensen, pp. 6-7. See also G. Jørgensen, *Den Danske Kirkes Historie for Hjem og Skole* (Copenhagen: H. Hagerups Forlag, 1914), pp. 149-150.

7. *Year Book, 1897* (Blair, Neb.: United Danish Evangelical Lutheran Church in America), p. 20. Danish-American churches succeeded in retaining only a small proportion of Danish immigrants within the Lutheran family. At the mergers of the 1960s, the UELC had 60,000 baptized members, the AELC 25,000. By contrast, the Norwegian-American churches which entered the new ALC numbered more than 1,100,000 baptized. Norwegian immigration was perhaps three times that of the Danes, but the Norwegian-background Lutheran churches in the U.S. were 13 times the size of the Danish-origin churches in 1960.

8. *Year Book, 1900*, p. 13.

9. *Year Book, 1897*, pp. 19-22. See also *Danske i Amerika* (Blair, Neb: Danish Lutheran Publishing House, 1900), 1:129-130.

10. Paul C. Nyholm, *The Americanization of the Danish Lutheran Churches in America* (Copenhagen: Institute for Danish Church History, 1963), pp. 95ff. See also Jensen, pp. 8-9.
11. Jensen, pp. 90-92.
12. *Year Book, 1904*, p. 100. The Norwegian Synod in 1903 had accused the United Church of being a sect and of false teaching in its doctrine of justification. The United Church appointed a committee to develop a documented response.
13. *Year Book, 1899*, pp. 24 and 53.
14. Jensen, pp. 220-221.
15. In the introduction to his history of the UELC, John M. Jensen writes (p. vi): "The pioneers had no help at all from the Church of Denmark. They were like the pioneers who cleared the forests and broke the prairie with their bare hands. Not a single theologian from Denmark came over to help them. . . . They literally had to train themselves to be pastors and missionaries in the new land."
16. Nyholm, pp. 41-42.
17. The United Church was also a leader among U.S. Lutheran bodies in its readiness to bring women officially into the work of the church. From early in the 20th century women held offices in congregations and were among the delegates to annual conventions.

## *Chapter 8*

1. For a recent survey of the emigration from Norway to the United States, see Ingrid Semmingsen, *Norway to America: A History of the Migration* (trans. Einar Haugen; Minneapolis: University of Minnesota Press, 1978). Two works by Theodore Blegen remain standard: *Norwegian Migration to America, 1825-1860* (Northfield, Minn.: Norwegian-American Historical Association, 1931) and *Norwegian Migration to America: The American Transition* (Northfield, Minn.: Norwegian-American Historical Association, 1941).
2. For a penetrating study of the intentions of those who formed the political structure into which the Norwegians entered in America see Martin Diamond, "Democracy and *The Federalist*: A Reconsideration of the Framers' Intent," *American Political Science Review* 53 (1959): 52-68.

3. A brief study of the background is provided by Einar Molland, *Church Life in Norway, 1800-1950* (trans. Harris Kaasa; Minneapolis: Augsburg Publishing House, 1957). A more detailed study by the same author is *Norges Kirkehistorie i det 19. Aarhundre,* 2 vols. (Oslo: Gyldendal Norsk Forlag, 1979). See also Andreas Aarflot, *Norsk Kirkehistorie,* vol. 2 (Oslo: Lutherstiftelsen, 1967).

4. On denominationalism, see especially "Denominationalism: The Shape of Protestantism in America," in Sidney Mead, *The Lively Experiment* (New York: Harper & Row, 1963).

5. I have depended throughout on the standard history of Norwegian-American Lutheranism by E. Clifford Nelson and Eugene L. Fevold, *The Lutheran Church among Norwegian-Americans,* 2 vols. (Minneapolis: Augsburg Publishing House, 1960).

6. The text of Oftedal's "Aapen Erklaering" is reprinted in Andreas Helland, *Augsburg Seminar gjennem Femti Aar, 1869-1919* (Minneapolis: Folkebladet Publishing Companys Trykkeri, 1920), pp. 440-442.

7. E. Clifford Nelson, *The Lutheran Church among Norwegian-Americans,* 2:42.

8. For commentary on the divisive issues written by an adherent of the Old School, see J. A. Bergh, *Den Gamle og Nye Retning eller Forsøg til Bedre Forstaaelse af Striden i Konferentsen* (Chicago: "Vort Land"s Trykkeri, 1884).

9. Paul G. Sonnack, "The 'United Church'; A Comprehensive Sense of Mission," in *Striving for Ministry* (ed. Warren A. Quanbeck; Minneapolis: Augsburg Publishing House, 1977), p. 101. A brief and insightful introduction to the election controversy is included in Eugene L. Fevold's "Coming of Age, 1875-1900," in *The Lutherans in North America* (ed. E. Clifford Nelson; Philadelphia: Fortress Press, 1975), pp. 313-325.

10. See Nelson, *The Lutheran Church among Norwegian-Americans,* vol. 2, ch. 5, for the final states of the controversy; the text of the Madison Agreement is in 2:356-358.

11. Peer Strømme, *How Halvor Became a Minister* (trans. Inga Bredesen Norstog; Minneapolis: Augsburg, 1936), p. 191.

12. Quoted in Nelson, *The Lutheran Church among Norwegian-Americans*, 2:24-25. At the time of union in 1890, the United Church counted 830 congregations—379 from the Conference, 268 Anti-Missourian Brotherhood, 41 Norwegian Augustana Synod, and 31 independents. Its 152,000 members represented roughly half of the Norwegian-American Lutherans.

13. For a detailed study and the continuing history see Eugene L. Fevold, *The Lutheran Free Church: A Fellowship of American Lutheran Congregations, 1897-1963* (Minneapolis: Augsburg Publishing House, 1969).

14. On St. Olaf College see Joseph M. Shaw, *History of Saint Olaf College, 1874-1974* (Northfield, Minn.: St. Olaf College Press, 1974).

15. Shaw, p. 15.

16. Shaw, p. 81.

17. Shaw, p. 17.

18. Ibid.

19. If St. Olaf College and the United Church have been accurately assessed here, their histories put a question mark against H. Richard Niebuhr's claim that inheritors of Luther's thought find Christ and culture to relate paradoxically. See Niebuhr's perennially stimulating *Christ and Culture* (New York: Harper & Brothers, 1951), especially pp. 149-189.

20. See Sverdrup's "Humanismen og Presteuddannelsen," in *Samlede Skrifter i Udvalg*, 6 vols. (Minneapolis: Frikirkens Boghandels Forlag, 1910), 3:214-225.

21. See, for example, *Report . . . Norwegian Lutheran Church of America . . . 1925*, pp. 67-69.

22. "Relationship of Schools, New Church Studied," *The Lutheran Standard* (October 7, 1983), p. 23.

## Chapter 9

1. N. N. Rønning, *Fifty Years in America* (Minneapolis: The Friend Publishing Company, 1938), p. 147.

2. Ibid, p. 146.

3. Andreas Helland, *Georg Sverdrup: The Man and His Message* (Minneapolis: Messenger Press, 1947), p. 47.

4. Herman Preus, "Syv Foredrag om det Religios Forhold i Amerika," *Luthersk Kirketidende* [Kirkelig Maanedstidende], July 1867.

5. Helland, p. 47.

6. Rønning, pp. 145-146.

7. For one comprehensive review, see Eugene Fevold, *The Lutheran Free Church* (Minneapolis: Augsburg Publishing House, 1969).

8. J. A. Bergh, *Den Norsk Lutherske Kirkes Historie i Amerika* (Minneapolis: Augsburg Publishing House, 1914), p. 368.

9. Eugene Fevold, *The Lutheran Free Church*, p. 99.

10. Carl Chrislock, *From Fjord to Freeway* (Minneapolis: Augsburg College, 1969), p. 12.

11. Georg Sverdrup, *Samlede Skrifter i Udvalg*, 6 vols. (Minneapolis: Frikirkens Boghandels Forlag, 1909-12).

12. Hogstad went to Madagascar in 1888, the first missionary sent overseas by a forerunner of what is now The American Lutheran Church.

13. Melvin Helland, trans., *The Heritage of Faith: Selections from the Writings of Georg Sverdrup* (Minneapolis: Augsburg Publishing House, 1969), pp. 4-5.

14. Fevold, p. 148.

15. One of the best poems by a Norwegian-American is an elegy for Sverdrup by Wilhelm Petterson, a teacher at Augsburg: "Nu rammer du haardt, du grumme død."

# Bibliography

## A. General U.S. Lutheran History

Bonderud, Omar, and Lutz, Charles, eds. *America's Lutherans.* Columbus: Wartburg Press, 1955.

Gremmels, Robert C. *Unity Begins with You.* Columbus: Wartburg Press, 1958.

Nelson, E. Clifford, ed. *The Lutherans in North America.* Philadelphia: Fortress Press, 1975.

Tietjen, John H. *Which Way to Lutheran Unity?* St. Louis: Concordia, 1966.

Wentz, Abdel Ross. *A Basic History of Lutheranism in America.* Philadelphia: Muhlenberg Press, 1955.

## B. German-American Lutheranism (former ALC)

### 1. General

Buehring, P. H. *The Spirit of the American Lutheran Church.* Columbus: Lutheran Book Concern, 1940.

Meuser, Fred W. *The Formation of the American Lutheran Church.* Columbus: Wartburg Press, 1958.

Schaaf, James L. *Wilhelm Löhe's Relation to the American Church: A Study in the History of Lutheran Mission.* Heidelberg: published by author, 1961.

Schmauk, Theodore E. *History of the Lutheran Church in Pennsylvania, 1638-1820.* Philadelphia: General Council Publication House, 1903.

### 2. Ohio Synod (Chapter 1)

Allbeck, Willard. *A Century of Lutherans in Ohio.* Yellow Springs, Ohio: Antioch Press, 1966.

Burgess, Ellis Beaver. *Memorial History of the Pittsburgh Synod of the Evangelical Lutheran Church, 1748-1845-1924.* Greenville, Pa.: Beaver Printing Co., 1925.

Peter, Martin Luther. *Aurora Community*. Aurora, W.Va.: Farm Women's Club, 1950.

Sheatsley, C. V. *History of the Evangelical Lutheran Joint Synod of Ohio*. Columbus: Lutheran Book Concern, 1919.

————. *History of the First Lutheran Seminary in the West*. Columbus: Lutheran Book Concern, 1930.

Stauch, Johannes. *Autobiography of Johannes Stauch*. German original in Lutheran Seminary Library, Gettysburg, Pa. English translation appears in Burgess' *Memorial History of the Pittsburgh Synod* and Sheatsley's *History of the Evangelical Lutheran Joint Synod of Ohio*.

### 3. Buffalo Synod (Chapter 2)

Denef, Ernst N. "History of the Buffalo Synod," *Wachende Kirche*, 1919-29. Buffalo. (German-language periodical of the Buffalo Synod.)

Grabau, Johannes A. A. *Tagebuch*, unpublished diary kept by Grabau during his 1837 imprisonment. Copies in the original and in English are held in the Archives of The American Lutheran Church, Dubuque, Iowa.

————. *Lebenslauf des ehrwuerdigen J. An. A. Grabau*. Buffalo: Reinecke und Zesch, 1879.

### 4. Synod in Texas (Chapter 4)

Biesele, Rudolph Leopold. *The History of the German Settlements in Texas, 1831-1861*. Austin: Press of von Boeckmann-Jones Co., 1930.

Heinrich, M. *History of the First Evangelical Lutheran Synod in Texas 1851-1926*. Chicago: Wartburg Publishing House, 1926.

Mgebroff, Johannes. *Geschichte der ersten Deutschen Evangelisch-Lutherischen Synode in Texas*. Chicago: Wartburg Publishing House, 1902.

Penniger, Robert. *Fredericksburg, Texas . . . The First Fifty Years*. Translated by Charles L. Wisseman Sr. Fredericksburg, Tex.: Fredericksburg Publishing Co., 1971.

Schick, Erich, and Haag, Klaus. *Christian Friedrich Spittler, Handlager Gottes*. Giessen: Brunnen-Verlag, 1982.

Staub, Hans, ed. *Wir sind sein Werk. 125 Jahre Pilgermission St. Chrischona bei Basel*. Giessen: Brunnen-Verlag, 1965.

Ziehe, H. C. *A Centennial Story of the Lutheran Church in Texas 1851-1951*. 2 vols. Seguin, Tex.: South Texas Printing Co., 1951 and 1954.

## 5. Iowa Synod (Chapter 6)

Brown, Dee. *Bury My Heart at Wounded Knee*. New York: Bantam Books, 1970.

Deindoerfer, J. *Geschichte der Evangel.-Luth. Synode von Iowa und anderen Staaten*. Chicago: Wartburg Publishing House, 1897.

Fritschel, Erwin. "A History of the Indian Mission of the Lutheran Iowa Synod, 1856 to 1866." Dissertation, Colorado State College of Education, 1939.

Graebner, Theodore. *Church Bells in the Forest: A Story of Lutheran Pioneer Work on the Michigan Frontier, 1840-1850*. St. Louis: Concordia Publishing House, 1944.

Keiser, Albert. *Lutheran Mission Work among the American Indians*. Minneapolis: Augsburg, 1922.

Krebs, Carl. "Selbstbiographie des Indianermissionars Carl Krebs." Unpublished manuscript. Abschrift im Archiv des Missionswerks Neuendettelsau, West Germany, Nr. 41-42 "Krebs." N.d. Unpublished trans. by G. M. Schmutterer.

Schmidt, Jakob. "Aus dem Tagebuch des Missionars Schmidt in Nordamerika." *Missionsblatt*, March–November 1859. Unpublished trans. by G. M. Schmutterer.

Schmutterer, G. M. "Pioneer Missionaries on the Western Frontier." Sioux Falls, S. Dak.: 1979. Unpublished manuscript.

Steward, Edgar I. *Custer's Luck*. Norman: University of Oklahoma Press, 1955.

Sunder, John E. *The Fur Trade on the Upper Missouri, 1840-1865*. Norman: University of Oklahoma Press, 1965.

Zeilinger, G. J. *A Missionary Synod with a Mission*. Chicago: Wartburg Publishing House, 1929.

## C. Norwegian-American Lutheranism

### 1. General

Bergh, J. A. *Den Norsk Lutherske Kirkes Historie i Amerika*. Minneapolis: Augsburg Publishing House, 1914.

Blegen, Theodore C. *Norwegian Migration to America, 1825-1860.* Northfield, Minn.: Norwegian-American Historical Association, 1931.

————. *Norwegian Migration to America: The American Transition.* Northfield, Minn.: Norwegian-American Historical Association, 1940.

Molland, Einar. *Church Life in Norway, 1800-1950.* Translated by Harris Kaasa. Minneapolis: Augsburg Publishing House, 1957.

Nelson, E. Clifford, and Fevold, Eugene L. *The Lutheran Church among Norwegian-Americans.* 2 vols. Minneapolis: Augsburg Publishing House, 1960.

Norlie, O. M. *History of the Norwegian People in America.* Minneapolis: Augsburg Publishing House, 1925.

Preus, J. C. K., ed. *Norsemen Found a Church.* Minneapolis: Augsburg Publishing House, 1953.

Quanbeck, Warren A., ed. *Striving for Ministry: Centennial Essays Interpreting the Heritage of Luther Theological Seminary.* Minneapolis: Augsburg Publishing House, 1977.

Rohne, J. Magnus. *Norwegian American Lutheranism up to 1872.* New York: The Macmillan Company, 1926.

Semmingsen, Ingrid. *Norway to America: A History of the Migration.* Translated by Einar Haugen. Minneapolis: University of Minnesota Press, 1978.

Syrdal, Rolf A. *White unto Harvest in China.* Minneapolis: Augsburg Publishing House, 1934.

## 2. Hauge Synod (Chapter 3)

Aarflot, Andreas. *Hans Nielsen Hauge—His Life and Message.* Minneapolis: Augsburg Publishing House, 1979.

*Budbaereren.* Periodical published by the Eielsen and Hauge Synods, 1868-1917.

Bull, Jacob B. *Hans Nielsen Hauge.* Christiania: Steen'ske Bogtrykkeri, 1909.

Gjerde, S. S. and Ljostvedt, P. *The Hauge Movement in America.* Minneapolis: The Hauge Inner Mission Federation, 1941.

Norborg, Sverre. *Hans Nielsen Hauge—Biografi 1771-1804.* Oslo: J. W. Cappelens Forlag, 1966.

———. *Hans Nielsen Hauge—Biografi 1804-1824.* Oslo: J. W. Cappelens Forlag, 1970.

Wee, M. O., and Rolvaag, O. E., ed. *Mindebok om Hans Nielsen Hauge.* Minneapolis: Augsburg Publishing House, 1926.

**3. Norwegian Synod (Chapter 5)**

Grindal, Gracia, "The Sketchbook of Linka Preus." Unpublished manuscript, Decorah, Ia., 1984.

Larsen, Karen. *Laur. Larsen: Pioneer College President.* Northfield, Minn.: Norwegian-American Historical Association, 1936.

Koren, Elizabeth. *The Diary of Elizabeth Koren.* Northfield, Minn.: Norwegian-American Historical Association, 1955.

Ylvisaker, S. C., et al., eds. *Grace for Grace: Brief History of the Norwegian Synod.* Mankato, Minn.: Lutheran Synod Book Co., 1943.

**4. United Norwegian Church (Chapter 8)**

Benson, William C. *High on Manitou: A History of Saint Olaf College, 1874-1914.* Northfield, Minn.: St. Olaf College Press, 1949.

Brun, N. C. *Fra Ungdomsaar: En Oversigt over den Forenede Norsk Lutherske Kirkes Historie og Fremskridt i de Svunde Femogtyve Aar.* Minneapolis: Augsburg Publishing House, 1915.

Dahl, T. H. *Den Forenede Kirke: Fred og Strid eller Lidt Forenings- historie.* Stoughton, Wisc.: Normannen's Trykkeri, 1894.

Norlie, O. M. *Den Forenede Norsk Lutherske Kirke i Amerika.* Minneapolis: Augsburg Publishing House, 1914.

Shaw, Joseph M. *History of Saint Olaf College, 1874-1974.* Northfield, Minn.: St. Olaf College Press, 1974.

**5. Lutheran Free Church (Chapter 9)**

Carlsen, Clarence. *The Years of Our Church.* Minneapolis: Lutheran Free Church Publishing Company, 1942.

Chrislock, Carl. *From Fjord to Freeway: 100 Years of Augsburg College.* Minneapolis: Augsburg College, 1969.

Fevold, Eugene. *The Lutheran Free Church: A Fellowship of American Lutheran Congregations, 1897-1963.* Minneapolis: Augsburg Publishing House, 1969.

Helland, Andreas. *Georg Sverdrup: The Man and His Message.* Minneapolis: The Messenger Press, 1947.

Sverdrup, Georg. *The Heritage of Faith: Selections from the Writings of Georg Sverdrup.* Translated by Melvin Helland. Minneapolis: Augsburg Publishing House, 1969.

## D. Danish-American Lutheranism and the UELC (Chapter 7)

*Femogtyve Aar, et Festskrift.* Blair, Neb.: Danish Lutheran Publishing House, 1921.

Jensen, John M. *The United Evangelical Lutheran Church: An Interpretation.* Minneapolis: Augsburg Publishing House, 1964.

Jørgensen, G. *Den Danske Kirkes Historie for Hjem og Skole.* Copenhagen: H. Hagerups Forlag, 1914.

Loft, Stinus S. *The Inner Mission Movement in Denmark.* Pamphlet.

Nielsen, H. Skov. *Dana College and Trinity Seminary: A Retrospect over a Half Century of Usefulness and Growth.* Blair, Neb.: Jubilee Booklet, 1936.

Nyholm, Paul C. *The Americanization of the Danish Lutheran Churches in America.* Copenhagen: Institute for Danish Church History, 1963 (distributed by Augsburg Publishing House, Minneapolis).

Vig, P. S. *Danske i Amerika I.* Blair, Neb.: Danish Lutheran Publishing House, 1900.

———. *Dansk Luthersk Mission i Danmark i Tiden før 1884.* Blair, Neb.: Danish Lutheran Publishing House, 1917.

———. *Trinitatis Seminarium.* Blair, Neb.: Danish Lutheran Publishing House, 1911.

*Year Books,* 1897-1904. Blair, Neb.: Danish Lutheran Publishing House.